THE WINNING WEEKEND WARRIOR:

How to succeed at golf, tennis, baseball, football, basketball, hockey, volleyball, business, life, etc.

John Charles Thomas, Ph.D.

THE WINNING WEEKEND WARRIOR: HOW TO
SUCCEED AT GOLF, TENNIS, BASEBALL,
FOOTBALL, BASKETBALL, HOCKEY,
VOLLEYBALL, BUSINESS,LIFE, ETC.

Dedicated to all of the weekend warriors, and especially to my favorite weekend warrior: Wendy Kellogg.

CONTENTS

ACKNOWLEDGEMENTS

The vast majority of sports books focus on one specific sport. In this book, I try to provide advice on sports, *in general,* while choosing examples from many sports. I would have had no chance at doing this except for the generous advice of many early readers who were familiar with various sports. Thanks in this regard go especially to Rory Stuart, Harold Toussiant, David Thomas, Wendy Kellogg, Tracee Wolf, and Carly Guiducci for their numerous suggestions and corrections.

I also received considerable good advice from Andrea Glass (www.writersway.com) and from the folks at Amazon.

This is a book based on a lifetime of passionate involvement with amateur sports. There would be no such experience to draw on without the thousands who joined me in my many sports-related struggles. Whether they were playing partners, competitors, coaches, spectators, commentators, or inspiring pros, they have all contributed to this book. Thank you!

PREFACE

I have greatly enjoyed sports as long as I can remember. As a child, I was blessed with good eye-hand coordination, but below average running speed. I had some early success with badminton, baseball, and dodge ball. Later, I enjoyed basketball, track, football, tennis, table tennis, softball, and golf. Although I enjoyed all of these sports, I never had illusions about being a professional athlete. Well, not too often.

Somewhere along the way, I managed to find time away from sports activities long enough to earn a Ph.D. in psychology and embark on a long career in a field called, "Human Computer Interaction." This field (also called "User Experience") basically tries to make sure systems are designed so as to be useful and usable by the people who use them. (Imagine!) I also found myself in a number of management and executive positions as well as working as a counselor and licensed psychologist.

In sports, I found myself winning on many occasions against people who were bigger, stronger, faster, more athletic, and often much younger. Over time, it seemed to me that many of my victories sprang from a few common themes repeated over and over. Many of these themes had to do with psychology and with management. Moreover, many of the ineffective decisions I saw people making on the golf course, the tennis court and the softball field bore a striking similarity to the ineffective decisions I saw people making in boardrooms, meeting rooms, and in software development projects. Indeed, seeing and overcoming many of these same human foibles formed the basis for the psychotherapy I practiced.

I began to wonder whether a book could help people become aware of some of these foibles and overcome them. If successful, such a book should aid people in *every* sport. For that matter, these same principles should help them in every other aspect of life. In this book, I have almost exclusively illustrated my points with sports. In a few cases though, I could not help myself from making comments about business. If you do not care about business, please feel free to skip right over those sections. Similarly, if examples from any particular sport leave you cold, please skip over those as well. Above all, this is a book, like sports itself, that is to be *enjoyed.*

CHAPTER ONE: WHY THE "WINNING WEEKEND WARRIOR"?

Your time is valuable! Why should you read this book which is general as opposed to specific books about tennis, football, baseball, basketball, and so on?

This book is valuable to you for several reasons. First when it comes to winning, there is much in common among all sports. In terms of the mental game, the commonalities outweigh the differences. In terms of the physical game, there are also great similarities in terms of preparation. Obviously, different sports require specific skills but these are largely improved due to *correct* practice in the specific sport. You can practice a sport such as golf or tennis for many years and hardly improve at all. Time alone is not enough. You need correct practice and this book can help you make sure you practice correctly.

A second reason to read this book is that even if you concentrate on one or two sports, chances are that you will participate occasionally in others. You may be a scratch golfer or a tennis star but occasionally find yourself in a basketball or baseball game. Even if your own days of playing hockey, tackle football and soccer are over, you might volunteer to coach these sports for kids, neighbors, or grandkids. In such cases, this book will help you *translate* the skills you already have in your main sports into these other domains. As you may have noticed, this is not always easy to do. Perhaps you managed to watch the basketball player, Charles Barkley (career average 22.1 points per game) struggle mightily to become a so-so golfer. You can also apply much of the advice in this book to business and other aspects of life far beyond sports.

A third reason to read this book is that thinking about what it takes to win in sports in general, will reveal additional insights helpful in your particular sport or sports. This is because I will ask you to look at sports through a different lens. Rather than look at baseball through a "baseball lens" and tennis through a "tennis lens" I will ask you to look at these sports through a more general lens.

The fourth reason is that reading this book provides an excellent foundation for understanding and using the information you may find in sports-specific books including future books in this series. By learning a general framework for thinking about all sports, other advice and tips will make more sense and be easier to remember and apply.

Fifth and finally, this is one of the few sports books written by a winning weekend warrior. I love competing in sports, but I have never been a professional athlete. Of course, you are tempted to read a book written by a world expert in a sport. Aren't we all? There are several problems trying to improve your performance based solely on books written by world class athletes. 1) There is probably no way you can keep your day job and keep to the kind of training schedule they have. 2) Most professional athletes are in their 20's and 30's. As you age, even if you keep fit, you may have to play differently compared to a professional athlete. 3) Most professional athletes have so much skill in their sport that they no longer consciously remember what the real issues are for beginners and intermediates. Many of these same limitations apply when we listen to athletes being interviewed by the press after an important victory (or defeat).

CHAPTER TWO: WHAT CAN YOU LEARN FROM INTERVIEWS WITH PROFESSIONAL ATHLETES?

How many times have you seen this? Popular "Pappa" Polozza is being interviewed about his recent phenomenal success. Of course, you and I would like to know what he did so we can do the same. Among his pearls are the following: 1) I just took it one play at a time. 2) I've been working really hard with my coach on refining my technique. 3). I've been really lucky to stay very healthy this season. Imagine he had answered with the *opposite* comments. 1). I just took it seven plays at a time. 2). I've been very lazy working with my coach. 3).I've been really lucky to be injured all season. We watch this great star being interviewed partly in the hopes that we will learn some secrets that we can apply to our own games and thus improve our winning percentage. Good luck. This happens very seldom. Why? For several reasons. First, most professional athletes are not that accurate in describing or explaining what they actually do. Part of the very reason that they are so good is that they are much more into the feel of what they are doing than the words or description of what they are doing. Suppose I interviewed you on TV and asked you: "How do you make your heart beat? How do you manage to breathe every day and even when you are asleep at night? How do you get your white blood cells to come out and kill germs when you are sick?" You do all these things and you do them well. But you cannot explain them.

Second, if you were earning tens of millions of dollars a year as one of baseball's most powerful home run hitters and you *could* explain your swing so well that a hundred thousand listeners could now go out and do the same, *would* you? Seriously? Why? If you would, fine, and by the way send me all your cash now. But most people would not give away real secrets that allow them to be champions even if they could.

Third, most of us do not have the body of a 22 year old professional athlete. We don't have the time to train 20-50 hours a week. As a result, even if you could swing a golf club as fast as Tiger Woods could in his (first?) prime, you would probably only do it once. Then you would strip a gear, throw a rod, or otherwise injure yourself. In addition, many world class athletes have some talents that cannot really be taught. Ted Williams (the Boston Red Sox slugger with a lifetime batting average of .344) had 20/10 vision. That means he could see details of the baseball and the pitcher's motion from twice as far away as a person with normal "perfect" vision. I have not heard this about the tennis star Novak Djokovic but I have seen him consistently correctly challenge the line judge on balls that were out by a half inch. And he accomplished this from the far side of the court. His vision is definitely better than mine ever was! I

5

was blessed to be born with flat feet and pronated ankles. This confers a definite disadvantage when it comes to running fast and jumping high. It does not mean I cannot run fast or jump high, but it reduces the chances of ever becoming a world class athlete in many sports.

This does *not* mean you and I cannot improve our games *considerably*. But it does mean we are not likely to get that improvement from watching professional athletes being interviewed. Buying this book is a much better step in the right direction. Reading it will help still more. Following the suggestions given and working on the exercises will help still more.

Of course, it is still *fun* to listen to top athletes. Such interviews are interesting, and even inspiring. On rare occasions, something does slip out that will be useful to you. But that might happen on "CSI" or "Breaking Bad" as well. Books and interviews written by world class athletes can be very interesting indeed for all sorts of reasons. But do not expect that you will gain much insight into how *you* can improve your winning percentage.

While many sports announcers are endlessly entertaining because of their humor or enthusiasm, many do not fare much better in terms of advice to help the weekend warrior. Without exaggeration, the following are very close paraphrases of some of the "sage pronouncements" I have heard from the coverage of various sports. Golf: "Well, yes, but he hit a lot of putts today that just missed the cup by inches, so, you know, when you putt like that you are close. You are just missing." "I think the reason he is down in this match is he just had to hit more shots than his opponent." "One thing I am sure that would have improved her score would be if she had sunk more putts." Football: "Why are they behind? Well, too many turnovers. You know, it is hard to win if you keep throwing interceptions and fumbling the ball." (As player is being carried off the field on a stretcher): "Well, that was quite a hit." Baseball: "I think the main reason the Yankees are winning today is that Boston just can't seem to hit what the Yankee pitcher is throwing." Basketball: "Duke is ahead because, basically, they have scored a lot more points." Marathon: "Here we are at mile 22. Frankly, the leader looks a little tired." Olympic weight lifting: "He couldn't quite get that clean and jerk. But you know, 435 pounds is heavy." Tennis: "Well, I don't think she is going to be very happy about double faulting[1] three times in one game." "These stats right here tell the story. They have both made the same number of unforced errors, but Serena hit twice as many winners. So, that's probably one main reason she's ahead."

---

[1] In tennis, the server gets two chances to hit a serve into the correct quadrant of the opponent's court. If they miss both, it is called a "double fault" and the receiver wins the point.

7

Of course, it is true that sometimes sportscasters *do* say instructive things; but it depends a lot on the particular sportscaster. When they do say instructive things, it is often quite particular to the situation at hand for those professionals in that particular tournament at that particular moment. It certainly enhances our enjoyment of watching the sport but does not offer much in the way of take-home lessons for the amateur.

PART ONE: STRATEGIC CONSIDERATIONS

I divide this book into two main sections: Strategic Considerations and Tactical Considerations. Strategic considerations are broader and more long term. Strategies determine how you choose and handle your sport, your training, and your practice. Tactical considerations are narrower and focused more on the short term. Tactics guide preparing for a particular match, game, tournament or contest. Clearly, many strategic and tactical considerations are about specific sports but a surprising number of them apply across sports (and other competitive domains as well).

CHAPTER THREE: WHAT DOES "WINNING" MEAN TO YOU?

Before tackling any campaign, you clarify your goals. At first glance, you may think that what "winning" means is obvious and does not really require any thinking. You want to score more points than your opponent and win. True, that is certainly one goal, but you need to think about that more deeply. One way to achieve *just that* is to find a player who is much much weaker than you are in a particular sport and then only play them. You should be able to win every single time. But would you really be satisfied? Probably not, I am guessing, because you actually have a number of other reasons for playing. You may be playing to improve your skill. You may be playing partly for the social benefits. You may be playing to get in shape — to feel better, look better, and live longer. You may enjoy the challenge of winning. If you only play the weakest player you can possibly find, you may always score more points but you will not improve your skill much; you will not make many new friends; and you will not be getting in shape as much as you would if you played a more challenging opponent; and the game itself may not be much fun.

Before you can decide on the right strategy for you to achieve your goals, you really have to understand what your goals are. How important are the various goals listed above? What other goals do you have beside the ones listed above? For example, do you prefer to play with the same small group of "compatible" friends and acquaintances or would you get more enjoyment out of continually meeting and competing with new people? Or, would some combination suit you best? How satisfied would you be if you continually compete against better players and improve your skill while your percentage of games actually won stays below 50%? How important is the setting of the game? For some people, it is important to play golf on a beautiful, well-maintained course. Others do not care that much. How important is it to use sports as an opportunity to get in better shape? If you find a tennis player who moves you from side to side on the court and plays drop shot after lob[2] and returns everything, you may find it difficult to win matches but at the same time, you will find yourself getting in much better shape. Improving in any sport, no matter what the method, will take some time and resource. How many hours a week are you willing to play and to practice? Even with minimal time, you can improve your wins by reading this book, thinking about the principles and applying them. Naturally, if you put more hours into play and practice, you will gain even more. How much time effort and money are you willing to put into finding a *good* instructor for you? Are you willing to change your habits in order to *eventually* play at a higher level?

The idea of being a winning weekend warrior is, of course, to be a winning weekend warrior and not to be forever lost in self-reflection like Hamlet! However, you will find it worthwhile to spend some time thinking about why you are interested in winning and what it means to you. This can be different for different sports. Perhaps you run in order to get in shape and you have no desire whatever to compete in races. You might play tennis mainly to win matches. And, maybe you play golf mainly for the social companionship and to be in beautiful venues. It is not necessary that

---

[2] A "drop shot" is a short shot that barely clears the net thus forcing the other player to run up to the net. A "lob" is a shot that goes high over the net and lands near the back line. If you can alternate the two effectively, you will force your opponent to run a lot.

you play every sport for the same reasons. Deciding for each sport what is important *for you* will help drive the strategic considerations. Understanding why you play each sport will help you choose opponents, venues, situations, and guide your training as well as your choice of instructor.

CHAPTER FOUR: PLAY TO YOUR
ADVANTAGES.

The ancient Greek philosopher Socrates reputedly
said, "know thyself." I was not around in the time
of Socrates and I do not read Greek either, but
let's just assume he *did* say that. It's good advice!
For you to increase your chances of winning, it is
really good advice. What are your relative
strengths? Do you run particularly fast? Do you
have lightning reflexes? Do you possess an
overwhelming drive to win? Can you control your
emotions when things go badly? Knowing your
strengths will help you choose your sports.

Joe comes to me for advice on how to be a better
gymnast. The first thing I notice is that he is over
6'8" tall, and weights about 240. I am thinking,
"Gee, Joe, why not become a jockey instead?" I
don't say that out loud but I do need to find out
why on earth Joe is even considering wanting to
become a gymnast instead of a basketball,
football, water polo, or volleyball player where his
size could be used to great advantage.

If you are fifty pounds overweight, you might find
tennis doubles more to your liking than singles. If
you have blinding fast running speed, that speed
provides an advantage in many sports including
baseball, basketball, football, track, tennis, soccer,
and lacrosse. However, it will not help you much in
golf, skeet shooting, table tennis, or croquet. It will
not *hurt* you to be fast, of course, but you might
chose sports that capitalize more on your talent.

Looking at the professional athletes in a particular sport is useful. Do you see any trends there? Professional football players tend to be big so that leads us to infer that being large is generally an advantage in football. On the other hand, professional soccer players tend not to be all that large. They are, however, lean and muscular, so if that describes you, you will probably do better in soccer than American football. You see remarkable golfers in just about all shapes and sizes so that tends to indicate that being of a particular body type is not a necessity to play golf quite well. Within one particular sport there are also differences depending on the position within the team. Baseball pitchers, catchers, and first basemen can be considerably heavier than center fielders or shortstops because the latter need to cover a lot of ground very quickly. Football receivers and safeties are faster and smaller than linemen. These are very important considerations for *professional* athletes. They may play *some* role in your choice of sports and positions. However, if your main goals are to have fun and lose weight, for example, maybe you prefer to play softball center fielder even if you are currently overweight. There is nothing wrong with doing so even if you would be unlikely to make the cut in that position on the Yankees or the Angels. If the most fun for you comes from winning and making the best possible contribution to the team, then, you might consider becoming a catcher, pitcher, or first baseman instead.

Of course, when it comes to knowing yourself, your mental characteristics weigh as heavily as your physical ones. In football, you can translate emotional frustration directly into physical energy by hitting harder and have good results. But that will not work at all in golf. In golf, you must be focused and determined but at the same time relaxed and confident. There are some sports in which good performance is based primarily on raw talent. It is quite possible that you might be big enough and strong enough to shot put farther than someone much smaller who practiced more. On the other hand, no matter how fast and coordinated you are, you will probably not execute a great pole vault your first time or play a great round of golf your first time out. An important consideration to understand about "knowing yourself" is to know how much practice you are willing (and able) to put into a sport.

Knowing yourself also includes knowing your situation. If you have job and family responsibilities that you need and want to keep up with, you may only have ten or even five hours a week to devote to your sport of choice. You might be *willing* to practice 40 hours a week, but it might be impossible, given everything else that is happening in your life. Your scheduling flexibility also matters. You can improve your biking, running, shot put, and discus on your own time while improving badminton, ping pong, and tennis requires a partner. To improve greatly in volleyball, soccer, football, basketball, hockey, or baseball, you need team practice. You need to be realistic.

CHAPTER FIVE: PLAYING THE FIELD VS.
PLAYING THE OPPONENT.

In some sports, you play against a very specific
individual or team. In other cases, you play against
the "field." In golf, for example, most tournaments
are known as "stroke play" and the person with the
lowest score among all the competitors wins.
Sometimes, however, golf is played as "match
play" and you play one specific opponent and win
"holes" whenever you score lower than that
specific opponent on that hole. These categories
of playing the field and playing the opponent
sometimes blend into each other. For instance, in
a 10K race or a marathon, there are so many
entrants that virtually everyone is competing
against the field. For many, "winning" is simply
finishing the race or establishing a new personal
best. However, sometimes a probable winner may
be mainly trying to out run a specific competitor
who is very likely to be the one person to beat.
Similarly, in a typical tennis tournament, the top
seeds must beat a series of less able opponents in
order to face each other in the finals.

I bring up this distinction because it once again
pays to have a clear idea of your goals. I was
recently taking an on-line course on corporate
strategy and one of the other students could not
understand the professor's explanation that it was
a good idea for a firm in a particular scenario to
lower prices in order to increase profits because
they would still be making less profit than their

"competitor." In business, your goal is typically to increase your own profit, not to "beat" your competitor. Often driving them out of business is the very worst thing you can do. It is worth noting that there can be multiple winners in business. Even when you are engaged in a competitive sport where there is only one winner, too much focus on "beating" your opponent is bad.

Let me give you an example. At the golf club in Westchester where I was long-time member, we held an annual tournament modeled after the Ryder Cup[3]. Essentially, we played a variety of formats for two days with the Blue Team against the Red Team. On the second day, I played a match against a much younger, stronger player who consistently outdrove me by at least fifty yards and sometimes by as much as seventy-five yards. Since this was "match play," in a sense, I had to beat this particular opponent. It would do our team no good for me to post an overall low score, if he beat me on more holes than I beat him. So, I was definitely playing this opponent and not the overall field.

However, it was still worthwhile to avoid *trying to beat this guy on every shot.* Readers who have

---

[3] The Ryder Cup is a team event played every two years between an American and a European team chosen from the best players. There are a variety of formats, but in each a person or a twosome is playing against a specific person or twosome.

played golf will understand this, but if you have never tried, you will have to take my word for it. The *worst* thing I could try to do would be to try harder by swinging the club harder and forcing myself to hit my drives[4] as far as he could. Going "all out" like that might well work in the 1500 meters or in weight lifting, but in golf, it is a deadly approach. Swinging as hard as I possibly could *might* enable me to hit one driver shot in the entire match as far as he did. But on almost every hole, I would end up hitting into the rough or out of bounds, skying the ball, or dribbling it along the ground. I had to let this guy play his game while I played mine. I had to strategize about where I could hit the ball in order to get fewer strokes on a hole than he did, even though he was typically much closer to the green[5] after the first shot than I was.

For example, on the par five fifteenth, there is water all down the right edge and a large sand bunker straight ahead. He positively smoked his drive over the sand (a feat few of my opponents had ever accomplished) and landed a good 275

---

[4] In golf, the first shot on the longer holes is called a "drive" and hit with the club that is the longest, heaviest, and hardest to control.

[5] The green is a very smooth section of the course with very short grass where putts are made. This is where you want your ball to be in as few strokes as possible.

yards from the tee[6]. I knew that it would still probably take him two more shots to get to the green. If he chose to go for the green in two, he would still have to hit a long wood and risk the water on the right of the green or pulling it left of the green where the ground was uneven and would require a delicate chip toward the water. So, tempting as it was, I gave up on trying to hit a 280 yard drive and hit out to the left of the large bunker[7] into the fairway[8]. From this angle, I hit a nice three wood and put myself about a five iron from the green. If I hit a nice iron shot, I should be able to two-putt the green and par[9] the hole with an outside chance of a birdie[10]. My opponent decided to go for the green in two and ended up in the water. This ended up being the decisive hole. Losing the par five where his length seemingly

---

[6] In golf, the tee is the area from which the first shot is hit. The ball is typically placed atop a small wooden or plastic platform also called a tee.

[7] A bunker, also known as a "sand trap", is a sandy area sometimes difficult to hit out of. Most players want to avoid them.

[8] The fairway is an area with relatively smooth short grass. It is easier to hit a shot from the fairway.

[9] Par is the score a good golfer should make if they make no errors on a hole. This is the most common score among the pros and welcome but unlikely for most players.

[10] Birdie is one stroke fewer than a par. Getting a birdie is one reason golf is so addictive.

gave him such an advantage ended up making him upset as well and he did not do well on the sixteenth hole where I went up two with two to play. We both parred the par three 17th and the match was over. [11]

Numerous examples of *not* playing the actual opponent but playing an "ideal" opponent come from my experience in tennis. I have seen players who "hate" a particular kind of shot and they foolishly let their opponents know. Sometimes they show this with an expression; sometimes, they show it with body language; sometimes, they come right out and say it. Maybe I have to rush to get to a shot that drops much shorter than I anticipated and all I can do is slide my racquet under the ball at the last minute for a drop shot[12]. Maybe I win the point and maybe I do not. But my opponent makes it clear that he *hates* drop shots. Hmm. Of course, a sufficiently clever opponent could be faking me out; maybe he eats up drop shots and he is just trying to trick me into hitting a

---

[11] A round of golf consists of 18 holes. After 17 holes, I was "up" by two strokes so even if he won the 18th hole, I would still be ahead by one and therefore, the match was over.

[12] A "drop shot" in tennis barely clears the net and typically has back spin and sidespin. It is meant to bounce twice before reaching the service line (the horizontal line a little more than halfway back in the court). If the opponent is back near the baseline (the horizontal line at the back of the court) reaching a good drop shot is difficult.

lot of them. More often though, this is a genuine reaction. My opponents sometimes have a very clear image of how they imagine points "should go" and they play to that idealized scenario rather than to what is actually happening.

I am subject to the same difficulty of course! It often happens, especially in doubles, that one of the opponents mis-hits a volley on the frame and instead of a crisp return, the ball just bloops over the net short. This provides a great opportunity to win the point for our side, but only if I can immediately overcome my expectations of where the ball "should" have gone and realize where the ball has actually gone! If it takes too long to get to the *real* ball position, they will win the point.

CHAPTER SIX: THE TRUE NATURE OF AN OPPONENT.

What is an opponent? The English word "opponent" originates from the Latin "ob" meaning "against" and "ponere" meaning "place." Indeed, in many sports, you literally "face" your opponents. Their place is opposite yours or you have opposing territory to defend in football, soccer, basketball, rugby, tennis, table tennis, and many others. Your goals are not their goals. Their goals are to stop you from reaching your goals, right? Yes, but only at one level. You are trying to pitch the baseball so your opponent cannot get a hit. Ideally, you would like to strike a batter out. If they do manage to hit the ball, the fielders try to thwart the opponent from reaching base safely. So it is in every sport, *at this level.* But there are other levels as well. At these other levels, *you and your opponent are actually working together to achieve common goals.*

You may be thinking, "What? How are we working together?" You are working together in several ways. First of all, you cooperate in playing by the rules and in entering into a contest. You cooperate in this because only in this way can you really have fun and enjoy the competition. Suppose you are playing tennis, for example. Instead of serving from behind the baseline, you walk up to the net and from a foot away, smash the ball down into the court so that it bounces over the back fence. What would be the point? You would be violating the rules and making it so that your opponent cannot possibly return the ball. And, if you kept doing that, obviously everyone else would quit, and quite possibly have you committed as well. You cooperate with your opponent in that you both agree to "play by the rules."

In the 1950's, I was an avid Cleveland Indians fan. I didn't have much luck though. They typically lost to the New York Yankees. In 1954, the Indians finally did have an outstanding season, won the pennant, but lost in four games to the Giants. Sigh. Along the way, I did develop a respect for the Yankee talents. In 1956, I played hooky from school to watch the Yankees play the Brooklyn Dodgers in the World Series. Playing hooky was not something I did very often but I could not have picked a better day! Don Larsen pitched a perfect game! For those who do not know baseball, a "perfect game" is very rare and means that one pitcher faces 27 consecutive batters and every one of them makes an out. Not only are there no hits, but there are no walks and no errors either! Of course, the goal of the Brooklyn Dodgers was to get hits and walks and score runs. They were completely frustrated by Don Larsen in reaching their goals. But did they get angry and yell and scream at Don Larsen? Of course not. In fact, it is extremely rare in professional sports (and for that matter, even in amateur sports) for someone to lose their temper because their opponent plays extremely well.

When do people lose their tempers at their opponents? People lose their tempers when they think that the opponents are playing outside the boundaries of the game. In baseball, for example, you may throw so well that no-one can hit your pitches, but that will not outrage them. Throw a ball at the batter's head though and you may empty the benches! Spectators may be frustrated by an extremely one-sided victory but the losers will seldom lose their tempers along with the game. What does anger a team is when they feel that the other team cheated or intentionally tried to injure a player (outside or beyond the rules).

There is another way that you and your opponent are cooperating and that is by being part of a larger enterprise. In the case of professional sports, having a worthy opponent directly adds to your bank account! Suppose there were only one really good team of soccer, American football, basketball or baseball and every time that team went to play, it was a forgone conclusion they would win. How much would the fans enjoy that? Not much. They would stop watching in person and stop watching on TV. The salaries of the unbeatable team would plummet. As a winning weekend warrior, your monetary earnings will be very limited compared with a professional athlete; possibly zero. On the other hand, you and your opponent are still engaged cooperatively in being part of a larger enterprise. That enterprise is mainly about having fun and staying in shape. It is also about improving and enhancing your skills. You and your opponent are involved in teaching each other to be better.

You can improve your tennis skills, and even have some fun, by hitting against a wall. But to improve significantly, you need to play against opponents who challenge you in various ways. For example, let's say your opponent owns a lightning fast serve that you find very difficult to return. You need to learn to return that serve! You may have to anticipate more quickly by seeing the position of the toss or the angle of the racquet. You might need to lose weight and strengthen your legs so you can cover more court. You might just need lots of experience trying to return the serve. Perhaps you need lessons and drills in returning serve. Maybe you need to change what you are doing. For instance, you might only have time on some serves to "block the ball" back. You probably will not be able to take the racquet back and make your full, normal forehand or backhand swing.

It is important to realize that your opponent is *not* your enemy. Although people sometimes use words like "destroy" or "kill" the opponent, this is not actually what is happening. In the short term, you and your opponent work together to have fun and enjoy life more. In the long run, you and your opponent cooperate to make both of you more skillful and healthy. Finally, in order to win more games, it really helps to understand, respect, and empathize with your opponent. The more you can "tune in" to their actual patterns of play, the more you can anticipate and get a jump on their likely next moves. The impact of this varies from sport to sport of course. If you are playing stroke play golf, you are trying to shoot the lowest possible score and your actions will not vary much according to what your (numerous) opponents are doing. On the other hand, in baseball, soccer, football, basketball, tennis, lacrosse, field hockey, volleyball, table tennis, racquetball, squash, handball, hockey, or rugby, being able to better understand what your opponent is capable of doing gives you a significant edge. I have been amazed in tennis, for example, that some players do not even realize that they have been playing a left-handed opponent for the entire match! In softball pitching, I have seen folks walk to the plate with "home run" written all over their face. They are so determined to hit that first ball out of the park, it is relatively easy to force them pop up or strike out. In many sports, you need to "know your opponent." Perhaps the only more important thing is to know yourself.

CHAPTER SEVEN: KNOW YOURSELF —
ASSESS YOUR STRENGTHS.

In order to play your best in any game that
involves strategy, it can be a great asset to know
your own strengths. I already mentioned in chapter
four, knowing your strengths can help you decide
at which sports you are likely to excel. Knowing
your strengths can also help you choose which
venues are best for you in whatever sport you do
play. If your main strength in tennis is a lightning
fast serve, you may win a lot on any surface, but
you will do relatively better on a fast surface like
concrete or grass. If your golf drives are high and
long, and you like playing in the rain, you might do
relatively well in a rainy match against someone
who hits low drives that bounce along the fairway
or who gets upset whenever it is wet. If you are in
great physical shape, then you will do relatively
better in tournaments that require a lot of games in
quick succession. On the other hand, if you get
tired and sore after one match, you may do better
in formats (like weekly leagues) that allow you
plenty of recovery time.

Knowing your strengths not only helps you choose
sports and venues but also helps you win
particular tournaments and games. For example, if
you are playing slow pitch softball and you are a
good placement hitter but can only hit it out of the
ballpark one out of one hundred times, then going
to the plate and trying to hit a home run every time
is simply helping your opponents. Be realistic and
hit singles. Four singles in a row probably gives

your team two runs and two on with none out. Two strike outs followed by a home run followed by a strike out gives your team one run with none on and the inning is over for you. If the longest you can consistently hit a three wood is 180 yards and you have to carry 185 over the water to get to the green, it is pretty silly to imagine by "trying really really hard" you'll hit it 185 and get on the green.

Generally, weekend warriors tend to overestimate their abilities, but occasionally people also play over modestly. If you are playing tennis doubles and able to ace your opponents on a regular basis, go for a big first serve and a difficult to return second serve. I've seen many people waste first serves almost the entire match hitting perhaps *one* ace the whole time. If you do this, then, to avoid the dreaded double fault, you may simply poke your second serve into the box. This provides the returner a number of good options including hitting a drop shot, a sharply angled shot beyond your reach, an alley shot[13], an offensive lob[14] or the receiver can hit it with pace and speed directly at your partner at the net. Instead of hitting 100% of your power on the first serve, you should hit that first serve at 90-95% of your power. You will get a few aces and force many weak returns for your partner to put away. And instead of playing

---

[13] The "alley" in tennis is the part that is "out" in singles but "in" in doubles.

[14] An offensive lob is hit just out of reach of the net person and gives little time for the server to get to the ball.

your second serve at 40% power, you should hit that one at 80-85%. Yes, you may get a couple double faults, but overall you will win far more points than with a second serve that is easy to put away.

That said, in games like tennis which are highly interactive, it might well be worthwhile to hit a serve at 40% power *on rare occasions.* If you are mainly hitting your serve at 80-95% power, then a very rare soft serve might throw off your opponent. Even if they do indeed "kill" that serve, it will increase their uncertainty for all your other serves. This brings us to a good general point which is to play to your strengths, but not every single time. If you have a powerful, fast, forehand with a lot of pace, of course, you want to use that on most occasions, but if you can vary that sometimes with a slower, higher ball that is still deep or a sliced slow deep return, it will make that strong top-spin forehand even more of a strength.

Your advantages are numerous and you should take honest stock of them. These advantages come in many forms. And one kind of advantage can often lead to others. For instance, in tennis doubles, if you are very tall, it will be relatively difficult for your opponents to lob over your head. This means that you want to develop another advantage: an excellent overhead. If you are hard to lob over *and* you have an excellent overhead, this greatly reduces the number of options your opponents can play. On the other hand, if you are short and cannot jump very well, you may need to develop the ability to run back quickly and to hit excellent lobs as well as the ability to volley well from slightly farther from the net.

Of course, when I say that it is important to understand *your* advantages, this includes not only you personally, but also the advantages of your teammates in team sports. If you are playing fast pitch softball and your pitcher is the fastest in the league, your right handed opponents may well be hitting a lot of balls to right field. If you are the pitcher on a softball team and your defense ranges from outstanding to mediocre, you can alter your pitching to encourage batters to hit to the outstanding fielders. If you are playing basketball on a team where one player hits a good 20% more of their shots, then you and your teammates obviously want to set up for that person to be able to shoot a lot. In professional sports, this principle is well-understood, but it often seems to be ignored in the world of the weekend warrior. This is odd because in many cases, the differences among various teammates in a typical amateur league can be tremendous. Although a few baseball pitchers have slightly lower fielding averages, most major leaguers have averages above .900 and most well above .900. But in amateur softball, it is not unusual for teams to have players with fielding averages between .700 and .800, and even below! Hitting a ground ball to a major league infielder will almost always get you out, but in amateur ball, if you pick the right target, you may well reach base from a hard hit ground ball. If your football team possesses a great quarterback and wide receiver combination, this also makes your draw play stronger. If your basketball team includes outstanding rebounders, it makes going for the three-pointer a better play.

CHAPTER EIGHT: DEVELOP YOUR EDGE.

Knowing your strengths and using that knowledge to help choose sports, venues, opponents, shots and so on is vital. A related concept is to "develop your edge." Many people focus on overcoming their weaknesses. While some time spent on this is useful, you will get more out of spending time improving and developing one or two unique aspects to your game.

For example, if you are a baseball pitcher, perhaps your best pitch is a curve ball. Of course, there is something to be said for adding additional reliable pitches to your arsenal, but if you have a decent fastball and a good curve, you will probably gain more by making your curve ball curve more, gaining more control, or making it less obvious when you are throwing it. Similarly, if you are a tennis player with a good kick serve[15] and a dubious drop shot, you will probably be far better off putting more hours into further improving your kick serve by making it faster, higher kicking and by hiding the spin better. It would be good to own some kind of reliable drop shot but you are probably not going to play it very often while you will serve about half the time in singles.

In team sports, different team positions further emphasize specialization. If you are a center or forward in basketball, improving your rebounding

---

[15] A "kick serve" puts topspin on the ball making it bounce high.

will be more important than if you are a guard. Of course, you will have more opportunities in games and scrimmages to practice and you probably have natural talents along these lines —- which is why you are a forward or center! If you are a football center, is greater speed an advantage? Of course it is! But you want to focus on being stronger and improving your blocking more than on increasing your speed.

Beyond improving one or two particular skills that are a "normal" part of the game, you may find some particular edge that is unusual. This is probably even more important for the weekend warrior than for the professional athlete. If you are able to hit a tennis ball reliably with unusually heavy sidespin, this is not going to throw off highly skilled amateurs or professionals. They have had hours and hours of practice dealing with this kind of spin. But if you are a weekend warrior, you might find this kind of spin is very difficult for some of your opponents to deal with because they have not had much experience with it. I have seen many examples of different kinds of "edges" that people have used in 3.0 to 4.0 tennis[16]. One player hit almost every shot with an unusual amount of backspin. It was very difficult to adjust to. Another player ran around the backhand to hit every shot with the forehand and delivered it with very heavy topspin. This particular guy worked on

---

[16] Tennis players are rated on a scale from 1 to 7 with 1 being an absolute beginner and 6 being perhaps offered a Division I college scholarship.

his grip muscles a lot and had a huge forearm on the right side. This also enabled him to hit the shot almost entirely with his arm and he was thus able to change directions at the last minute. I played against several players who had very unconventional and "weak" volleys but on many shots at the net, they would hold the racquet in front of them and "poke" it at an extreme angle. This type of shot would not be powerful enough to win very often in high level tennis doubles but in 6.0 doubles[17], it was quite effective. Another tennis edge which I have used to great advantage myself is a lob with so much topspin that it becomes nearly impossible to return[18] except by hitting a swinging volley[19] or catching it on the rise.

In tennis, as well as other sports with a "serve" such as volleyball, table tennis, racquetball, and squash, having an *unusual* serve as well as a "good" serve is a great advantage for the winning weekend warrior. I have seen many kinds of unique serves in tennis that were winning advantages because they were unusual more than anything else. Of course, if you really are capable

---

[17] In tennis doubles, the ratings of the two players are added together to calculate the team rating.

[18] Because the lob basically bounces over the opponents head and into the fence behind them.

[19] A swinging volley is just that: a shot where the player hits a volley but with a full swing rather than the short swing of a normal volley.

of hitting rocket fast aces 60% of the time, that is a serve that is good and unusual. But I have also seen people who have effective serves because they land unusually short, are sharply angled, high bouncing, hit the tape, or even are hit underhanded. Some kinds of "edge" are more sustainable than others. If your "edge" is that you hit a lightening fast serve, that is going to be trouble for your opponents forever. Hitting the serve short, underhanded, or very high is going to throw many opponent's off for a time but then they will adapt to it. So, that is a kind of "edge" that will help a lot in a round robin tournament with strangers but not be much of an edge for very long if you keep playing with the same group month after month.

The importance of having a unique "edge" varies from sport to sport. In the 100 meters dash, you basically have to get out of the blocks quickly and run as fast as possible in order to cross the finish line first! The concept of "edge" does not play out the same in such sports because success boils down to speed. Similarly, in the shot put, you basically want to throw farther than anyone else. There are a number of skills needed and you need to train for strength in many muscles but all are important for maximum throws. Golf requires a great number of skills to play well, and all of them are important. If you want to do well as a weekend warrior, you need to be able to drive the ball in the fairway, hit good iron shots, chip, pitch, putt and hit sand shots. If you keep missing three out of four fairways, it will not matter how good the other parts of your game are. Similarly, if it takes you three or four shots to get out of the bunker, you will be in trouble unless you play non-optimal shots to make sure you never end up in one. And, if you three putt every green, you will not score well no matter how good the other parts of your game are. So, in golf, you really do need to develop all the skills up to a decent level. That said, many golfers spend far too little time improving their putting as compared with trying to add five to ten yards to their drives. If you want to do well at golf at your club, keep the ball in the fairway and putt well. If you quit your day job and turn pro, that's when it really becomes an advantage to hit 300 yard drives.

An edge in any sport can be novel. In fact, if you invent your own edge, it will be even more surprising for your opponent and more difficult for them to deal with. One way to create a novel edge is to exaggerate something that is already part of the game. For example, many tennis players can hit a serve with topspin or sidespin. You can create a novel edge by hitting the serve with a *tremendous* amount of topspin or sidespin. To the extent you can disguise and vary this, so much the better. If you are a softball pitcher, you may take something that currently exists such as a curve, sinker, rising ball, or knuckleball and exaggerate it so that it curves or sinks or rises or jerks more than your opponents are used to. Again, to the extent that you vary and disguise these, so much the better.

Another way to create a novel edge is to combine two or more elements. For example, in tennis if you can combine a short shot with backspin and sidespin, you can create a very effective drop shot. If you combine the ability to hit a good drop shot with the ability to hit a good topspin lob, you will quickly wear out all but the best conditioned opponents. Sometimes a player can introduce a completely novel element into the game and create an edge. This is often quite controversial, especially at first. Sam Snead, the first professional golfer to embrace the croquet style putt, became too good a putter! As a result, the style was banned. Fiberglass poles were at first outlawed in the Olympic pole vault but now they are used by virtually every vaulter. Baseball's "spitball" was too effective (and dangerous) in its surprises and so was banned although controversy remains about just how effective this "ban" really is.

The point is that introducing something really novel in terms of equipment or technique may well allow you to have an edge but at some point, the edge may be *too good.* That is, your advantage will result in your opponents objecting to your using it at all! You will have to answer for yourself in your own circumstances how much of a novel edge might be "too much." One novelty I have employed myself but which never caught on, is pre-hit defensive movement in slow pitch softball. In major league baseball, the pitching constrains the batter so much and the distances in the outfield are so great, that it makes perfect sense not to have outfielders running around on every pitch. It would not matter because no batter possesses the skill to hit the ball twenty feet one way or the other. Slow pitch softball is quite another matter. In slow pitch softball, a decent and patient hitter who is not silly enough to try to hit a home run at each at bat, should be able to direct the ball to any hole in the outfield. The fielders have plenty of time to move as the ball is pitched and still come to a ready position before it is hit. This should make the hitter's job much more difficult even if he does not take his eye off the ball to look at the fielders and try to change his target at the last second. But I never see a team employ this tactic. Some slow pitch softball players may be too out of shape to do this, but most are not. It would have the additional advantage of making the fielder more "active" right before the hit and probably result in more athletic running as well. I can only guess that it is too novel for most people's comfort level.

CHAPTER NINE: ASSESS YOUR WEAKNESSES.

While more attention should be paid to building on your strengths and developing your edge, some attention does need to be paid to assessing your weaknesses as well. This can be difficult for some people. Let me re-phrase that. This is difficult! One problem with the word "weakness" is that it might imply a characteristic that is unchangeable. In reality, almost any "weakness" is temporary. It can change as a function of practice, strength training, rules changes, environmental changes, and so on. What could be more permanent than the loss of a limb? Yet, even here, modern technology and medicine are making great strides with prosthetics. The point is that any weakness is best viewed as a temporary state. Assessing your weakness is a starting point; not an end point. Finding out what your current weaknesses are is the first step in an action plan. Making a plan and carrying out that plan will turn a "weakness" into an opportunity. Of course, this approach is not limited to sports alone. This same approach is true in your personal life, in business, in politics and so on.

In terms of sports, it is important to realize that there are many possible areas for improvement just as there are many possible sources of current strengths. You may have the opportunity to improve your basic underlying level of fitness by increasing your strength, your endurance, your flexibility, your balance, or your speed. There may be specific skills that need to be improved; for instance, your tennis backhand, your golf chipping, your ability to hit to the opposite field in softball, your basketball jump shot, or your ability to handle splits in bowling. You may have opportunities to improve your strategy and tactics. For example, you may score lower in golf if you try to make fewer miracle shots or stick to a specific repeatable routine on every single putt. In tennis, you may improve your winning percentage by learning to stay out of "no-man's land" (behind the service line but well inside the baseline) more consistently. In softball, your team will definitely win more games if you all try to get base hits instead of home runs at each at bat. Finally, you may find that an important opportunity for improvement is in the mental game. Staying positive when you are down in the score and learning to stay relaxed and focused regardless of circumstances are important and learnable skills for every sport.

In some cases, it will work best to address several opportunities at the same time. For example, in tennis, you may have the mental attitude that you "cannot" play the net very well so you avoid it at all costs and end up hitting many volleys from mid-court. You may play here because you are too slow to handle volleys closer to the net and because you don't have the speed to run back for a lob from closer in. By never approaching the proper net position, you have very little practice. So, on the rare occasions when you do move to a proper net position, you hit a shot that you have little practice with and no confidence in. As a consequence, you are likely to do poorly and this in turn, reinforces your idea that you "cannot" play the net. In a case like this, it will work best if you address this opportunity with a plan that addresses all of these inter-related issues at the same time. 1. Put in some training time and/or lose weight in order to become able to run back for a lob if needed. If this really is physically impossible, then for doubles, you need to find a partner who is capable of running back for lobs. 2. At the same time, you need to make a conscious effort to remember to approach the net and stay out of no-man's land[20]. 3. Mentally convince yourself that you are capable of playing closer to the net and that this skill will take time to develop. Even the pros miss volleys at the net occasionally so do not give up if a few volleys go astray. 4. Practice your skills. Drill on volleys at the net till you improve your skill and confidence. 5. Assess the situations. Just because you become more able at the net does not mean you should *always* play close to the net. If you are playing tennis doubles and your partner serves weakly, some opponents may find it a useful tactic to drill the ball back right at you. In this situation, it might make sense to play back until your partner develops a better serve or until you go up against a player with a weaker return. This does not invalidate your whole plan for staying out of no-man's land nor for

---

[20] In tennis, most shots should ideally be hit either from a position near the baseline at the back of the court, or fairly close to the net. The area in-between is called, "no-man's land." Shots hit from this area are difficult to execute.

taking the net more aggressively when it is justified.

Sometimes, assessing your opportunities for improvement requires some thinking. You might not diagnose the issue properly if you rush to judgment. For example, you may find yourself three-putting many greens. And, you may notice that you are missing half of your six foot putts. So, you decide, by golly, you are going to do something about this and practice six foot putts over and over. As it turns out, the pros on tour miss half of their six foot putts! So, sinking half of your six foot putts is not actually your problem! That is a strength! The real problem is that you hitting so many of your second putts from six feet. You need to practice your lag putting[21] so that almost all your second putts are from three feet or less. While it may seem as though the difference between sinking a six foot putt and a three foot putt is trivial, it turns out it is not.

Because diagnosis is difficult, it is often worthwhile to get the advice of a professional coach or teacher. They have a much better perspective because they have seen many players in your particular sport. Be careful though and pick a *good* coach or teacher. Beware of one that jumps to conclusions. A golf teacher, for instance, should watch you hit many shots before deciding what

---

[21] Typically, one is expected to hit two putts on a green. The first putt, which can be from fairly far away is called a "lag putt."

you need to change. I will say more about this in the chapter on choosing a coach but at this point, I want to point out that left to your own devices, you may solve the "wrong" problem. You may do even worse by listening to the advice of well-meaning friends. Even if they are better than you at a particular sport, they may be terrible at diagnosing how you can do better. Often, people will repeat advice they have heard or seen without any real analysis of whether it is true or if true, whether it is applicable to you.

Because golf allows intermittent play, it is perhaps the sport most prone to unsolicited advice. If you slice, hook, push, pull, or top the ball: "Keep your head down." If you leave a putt short: "Never up, never in." If your putt goes left of the hole, "You pulled it." And on and on go the analysis and implicit advice. Most golfers never knowingly subtract two strokes from their score on a given hole to change their bogie[22] to a birdie. Yet, they often fail to penalize themselves two strokes for giving unsolicited advice. It is *possible* that your putt missed left of the hole because you pulled it. But it is also possible that you misread the green[23] or the grain or that your putter head was not

---

[22] In golf, par is the score a good player is expected to get on a hole. Bogie is one more stroke. A birdie is one less stroke. (Fewer strokes are better!).

[23] The green is the smooth putting surface around the hole. Sometimes, the grass grows at an angle and this can affect the path of a putt.

square at impact. It is also possible that the North Wind, at that exact moment, sent a little puff of air to blow your ball off course. Golf is complicated and even with slow motion video, it is difficult to diagnose exactly what is going wrong and should never be done on the basis of a single shot. Certainly, a well-meaning friend is unlikely to be able to make an accurate and instantaneous analysis based on their naked eye observation. Moreover, even if their analysis, by some miracle of good luck is correct, it will probably *not* be to your advantage to try to take this advice to heart *during a round.* Of course, that is probably precisely why it is against the rules to give such advice.

Most coaches in most sports begin by analyzing you in an artificial situation such as a tennis lesson or on the golf driving range. If you can afford it, I would much rather have that pro watch you during actual play. Only then can they possibly prioritize what changes will have the most profound impact on your play and ability to win. What does it matter if you have a completely "abnormal" tennis serve if you are getting nearly every first serve in and getting an ace or two a game? What does it matter if you swing the golf club like Jim Furyk or blast the ball so hard you lose your balance like Bubba Watson if you win tournaments? Are these abnormalities the things to "fix"? I played on a slow pitch softball team with a decent hitter who swung the bat *vertically!* If you were a coach and you watched him hit, you might have a heart attack or stroke right then and there. If you were not rushed off to the ER, you might well try to fix this "horrible" swing. But in actual game play, he was effective in hitting and provided the additional advantage that for the first four or five innings, the other team was wondering what the blazes he was doing rather than concentrating on their own pitching, hitting and fielding. Similarly, I have had the pleasure(?) of playing golf against opponents whose swing was such an elaborate and un-athletic conglomeration of "mistakes" that it was agonizing to watch — even though they hit every fairway! "If it ain't broke, don't fix it." And knowing what is "broke" depends on seeing how it actually plays out in real contests. It is not enough to match a golf swing, or a basketball shot, or a high jump, or a tennis serve against some imaginary ideal *out of context.* In fact, some of these players actually might have developed exactly the kind of successful "edge" talked about in the last chapter only to have well-meaning pros treat that feature as a bug to be eliminated. The moral of the story is that it is important to assess your opportunities for improvement, make a plan and implement that plan. But — make sure you are making all that effort based on a careful analysis of what is actually going to help you win and not based on making your play superficially look more like the "ideal" play of a top-notch college or professional athlete.

CHAPTER TEN: THE IMPACT OF AGE.

In my first job after graduate school, I managed a research project on the psychology of aging at Harvard Medical School. We looked at the reaction times and memory performance of healthy males ranging in age from their twenties to their sixties. While there are some negative aspects of aging, it is a whole lot better than the only other available alternative! The "impacts" of "age" are really not so severe or as consistent as you might think. The differences *among* people in any one decade of age were much larger than the overall age-related change from the twenties to the sixties. Furthermore, the effects of the environment were larger even than individual differences. If you are a coach (or a leader, manager, or executive), making sure the situation is set up properly is much more important than finding an exact "talent match" for the situation. Unfortunately, in my experience, most companies put a lot more focus on selection than on making a good environment for people to work in. In the work environment, many of the "differences" in performance are purely arbitrary and imposed.

In athletics, however, we face a world which is *intentionally* made challenging and the situation *intentionally* exaggerates small differences in performance. If you were a human factors engineer and you wanted to improve performance in golf, it would be easy! You would design the fairways to be wider and shorter, the greens to be softer, and above all, make the holes much, much larger. In golf, however, and in all sports, the course is designed to be difficult *on purpose.* What is ironic is that many managers and executives design their work environments along similar lines *for no reason at all.*

Anyway, because sport situations are intentionally designed to be challenging, individual differences and age differences are exaggerated in their effects. Athletes are pitted against each other and often have to engage in multiple sequential contests in order to win a tournament. Since it takes a little longer to recover when people are older, this process makes it more likely for a young athlete to win. You may see a remarkable round or two of golf from a competitor in their fifties or sixties, but it is slightly more difficult for them to put together four such rounds in a row. Similarly, tennis tournaments require the eventual winner to play through several rounds in a few days with enough rest in between for a young player to recover completely but probably not enough time for an older player to recover completely. In contact sports like basketball, baseball, hockey, rugby, and football, the time between successive games is long enough for younger players to recover and practice but typically not long enough for an older player to do the same. In addition, the scoring systems for many sports exaggerate differences between players. For example, in tennis, if you win 60 % of the points and your opponent wins 40%, you will win far more than 60% of the games and way more than 60% of the sets and almost certainly win 100% of the matches (and not just 60%). Even within individual points of a tennis match, if you can push your opponent side to side a little farther with each shot than they can push you, after five or six shots they are running *much* farther from side to side than you are. A player with a consistent 130 miles per hour serve will not win 30% more aces than a player with a 100 miles per hour serve of the same consistency. They will probably hit 300% as many aces. The service box[24] is *designed* this way. If it were half the width then a good player could reach serves that were wide or down the T equally well at 100 miles per hour or at 130 miles per hour. If the net were twice as high, service aces, at least those based on speed and location, would pretty much drop to zero. Of course, the game would be less interesting as well. Precisely because service aces are *possible* but *difficult,* that part of the game holds drama.

We will probably never see the top ranked tennis player in the world, or the world's fastest sprinter, or the MVP basketball player be a sixty year old. That said, there is no reason that you cannot *enjoy* sports at every age. Moreover, the "impacts" that

---

[24] The serve must go over the net and into one of the quadrants of the court near the net in order to be "good." In the so-called "deuce" court, the server stands slightly to the right of the midline and behind the baseline and must make the serve bounce into the box on the near left side of the court. In the "add" court, the server stands slightly to the left of the midline behind the baseline and must hit the ball into the box on the near right side.

people often associate with age are primarily impacts, not of age, but of inactivity. Slowness, lack of balance, loss of strength, loss of muscle mass, loss of bone density, cardiovascular issues, and memory problems are *slightly* age-related issues but they are *strongly* related to lack of physical activity.

This does not mean that if you have been sedentary for years, that you should immediately go out and embark on an absurdly aggressive physical exercise regimen. And, obviously, whatever your age, should consult with your physician before making significant lifestyle changes. But it does mean that sports serve as a wonderful "antidote" to many of "hardships" that are often associated with age. As Christopher Alexander points out in *A Pattern Language,* "The human body does not wear out with use. On the contrary, it wears down when it is not used." His pattern 72, "Local Sports" focuses on the importance in urban planning for including spaces to support local sports.

Although evidence keeps mounting that engaging in physical activities will help you stay "young" healthy and mentally alert (as well as being happier), most sports situations are designed to exaggerate small differences. You can mitigate these effects and keep active in sports throughout life by choosing your sport, your venue, your opponents, doing what you can to train properly, and adjusting your strategy and tactics.

First, there are some sports such as the ones mentioned above: full contact tackle football, aggressively contact basketball, hockey, and rugby that probably will be mostly limited to people below their fifties. I do have a friend in his sixties who plays rugby though and is prepared to endure long recovery periods from broken bones. But for most people, there are a wide variety of sports than can be enjoyed in the fifties, sixties, seventies and beyond.

In many sports such as swimming, track, golf, triathlons, and tennis, there are masters or seniors categories so that people can compete in their own age category. Generally, people compete in younger (open) categories if they so choose. In some cases, age may influence your choice of venue. You might be in good enough shape to run a marathon at seventy, but you may want to pass on events where the temperature is in the 90's. Night vision is diminished with age so playing under dim lighting conditions disadvantages older participants.

Probably the single most important thing you can do to mitigate the effects of aging is to use proper training. While exercise is important when you are young, it is vital when you are "middle aged" and absolutely *critical* when you are older. Having professional advice is similarly even more important when you are older. You need to train but you also need to avoid over-training even more than when you are younger because your recovery time will be longer. Unfortunately, in my experience finding a good coach for an older athlete is not easy. On the one hand, they may be completely ignorant of how to modify exercises and exercise programs to make them age-appropriate. On the other hand, other coaches unknowingly limit your performance by assuming you are old and probably incapable of much or by focusing their time and attention on younger and "more promising" players. You may have to try out several personal trainers in order to find one who can "push" you appropriately.

In addition to practicing whatever sport or sports you want to play, in order to do your best as an older athlete, you need to supplement that practice with cardio training, strength training, flexibility exercises, and balance exercises. All of these take time, obviously, and that is another reason why it is really important to understand what "winning" means to you before you can design an optimal program for yourself. Yoga can provide a good way to work on flexibility and balance. Weight training is good for strength. Cardio training can include running, power walking, stair climbing, swimming, biking, cross-country skiing, soccer, or back-packing. Flexibility and balance can be worked on every day. You want to do weight training on any particular muscle group 2-3 times a week. Cardio should be done 4-7 days a week. All of this naturally presumes that you have gotten the go-ahead from your doctor and worked up to that kind of schedule gradually.

If you do all of these things, you can enjoy and win at many different kinds of sports regardless of age. You might further improve your "winning" percentage by altering your tactics and strategy slightly. How to do this in detail depends on the specific sport, but let's look at a few examples.

When you were in high school, you may have been a valuable basketball team member mainly because your jumping ability enabled you to capture a lot of rebounds. In your thirties, you may have still captured a lot of rebounds because your experience enabled you to jockey into the proper position more intelligently than when you were in high school even though you may have lost a few inches in your jump. In your fifties, however, you are probably not going to be an outstanding rebounder unless you are playing with other fifty-somethings. On a mixed age group team, you may need to further develop your accuracy for outside shots. In addition, your "unusual" high school height of six foot three inches is no longer "unusual" at all! This is not really an effect of "age"; it is an effect of generational changes.

In your twenties, you might have been an unusually good tennis singles player mainly because your speed and anticipation enabled you to run down everything. In your forties, this still provides a good area of focus if your opponents are of similar ages. However, if you want to win against players of all ages, you need to shift your focus and your tactics. Perhaps you can develop a lightning fast serve and volley game. In your seventies, however, serving fast enough to overwhelm younger opponents is probably no longer an option. You may need to work on court position, hitting deceptive shots and unusual spin. Or, you may decide it is time to switch to doubles. There may be real effects of age that you need to take into account, but you should not use age as an "excuse" when it is really lack of training or practice that is the issue. You may have had a very fast serve when you were thirty and now, at fifty you cannot generate the speed. Well, *maybe* that is due to age. But perhaps it is also true that when you were thirty, you played ten hours a week and then practiced your serve another four hours a week. Now, you play for three hours a week and do not practice your serve at all outside of a few warm-up serves before your matches. Your current lack of aces cannot properly be blamed on age! Practice that serve four hours a week for a month, do strength training and flexibility exercises, and if you see no improvement in speed, *then,* you might blame it on age and try to adjust your game accordingly by altering the spin, the placement, and making sure your posture and toss do not give away your serving intentions.

Of course, changes in one aspect of your game also may mean cascading changes in other aspects of your game. Your long time doubles partner may have put away many volleys at the net when you were serving hard twenty years ago. Now, he or she is making a lot of "mistakes" at the net. Is that because of slower net play reactions? Or is it because your serve is giving the opponents too much time to "tee off"? Whereas twenty years ago, you never found it necessary to "communicate" explicitly to your partner about your serve, maybe now you do. Perhaps you need to clue them in ahead of time on where you intend to serve or he needs to signal you whether they are going to try for an all out poach. Maybe they should occasionally play back or you should occasionally rush the net so the opponents are more off balance. The specifics vary from sport to sport, from team to team, and even from one situation to another. But the constant is that you need to be flexible in your approach and be willing to change as needed. But don't use age as an easy excuse for losing points that are really due to bad position, lack of adequate training or practice, or lack of communication with your teammates.

One final word on aging. Don't focus on it. It can become a very convenient excuse for lack of skill that is mostly due to lack of sufficient training, lack of practice, lack of a good coach or bad tactics. The human body largely regenerates itself constantly. Your blood, muscles and bones are not "sixty" or "seventy" or "eighty" years old. They are renewed all the time. Different types of cells replenish at different rates but even your "old bones" are likely no more than ten years old. In any case, keep a positive mental attitude. That is far more important than age.

CHAPTER ELEVEN: CHOOSE YOUR SPORTS.

The first thing to notice about the title of this chapter is that it says, "choose your sports" and not "choose your sport." Why? If you are a highly paid professional athlete, you really want to spend almost all your time in one particular sport and push as far as you can while you are in your prime. It is fine to enjoy other sports on occasion but you want to do that sparingly and carefully avoid a recreational injury that might jeopardize your career. On the other hand, if you are a weekend warrior who wants to win more often than you do, then you want to choose more than one sport.

There are several reasons for the weekend warrior to spend time on more than one sport. First, the effects of age explored in chapter ten impact which sports you excel in. Second, engaging in multiple sports allows you better insight into which ones really give you the most pleasure and which you are talented in. Third, by applying your natural creativity, you may find ways to improve in one sport based on another. Fourth, engaging in multiple sports will probably keep you in better all around shape than any one sport. Another reason is simply opportunity. Let us examine each of these factors in turn.

First, different sports have different peak ages for professional athletes. Baseball players tend to peak from 27-29. Within baseball, there are different peak ages for different skills. For example, base stealing peaks at a younger age than drawing walks. Tennis players tend to peak 20-25 while basketball stars peak at 27. Sprinters tend to peak in the lower to mid 20's while endurance runners peak at older ages. Golf performance tends to peak in the 25-35 age range. These figures are based on professional athletes. Judging the impact on the weekend warrior is trickier. Your own peak performance could differ wildly from these averages and, of course, a lot depends on whether you are competing with people of all ages or people that are roughly in your own age group. It may be true that the "peak" age for professional tennis players is in the 25-35 age range but some people can play and enjoy tennis into their 70's and 80's at least. Similarly, amateur golfers often play their *best* golf after retirement, mainly because they now devote the time needed to hone all the many skills of golf. The most important factor in choosing the sports to focus on is to pick sports that you enjoy. If you cannot or will not get over the frustration that necessarily accompanies golf, then that may not be the sport for you.

I would recommend that weekend warriors spend some time working on a sport that they can play for a long time as well as one that they can enjoy now. If you are in your twenties or thirties and enjoy playing soccer, rugby, or tackle football, that's wonderful. But your overall winning during your life will be increased if you also take the time to learn something like softball, tennis, swimming, running, or golf that you can enjoy for the rest of

56

your life. As I said, I do have one friend in his 60's who plays rugby but he is an exception. A bit of time acquiring the skills of other sports while you are still relatively young will make it much easier to excel at these sports later. It is certainly *possible* to first learn to golf when you are 70, but it will be easier if you take some lessons in your teens, twenties or thirties. Furthermore, if you learn to swing a golf club when you are young, you will know what it feels like to swing like a young person and this will help encourage you later in life to do the strength and stretching exercises needed to keep you swinging more youthfully. If you first pick up a golf club in your seventies, this will be harder to achieve (but by no means impossible).

The second reason to try out multiple sports and really try to excel at them is that you may find that the reality of playing a sport and the image of that sport are quite different. This is not just true of sports, of course. TV shows about being a policeman do not give you a very good idea of what it is like to *be* a police officer. Similarly, studying psychology is quite different from being a psychologist. It might look really cool when professional basketball players run, pass, and shoot. But that doesn't mean you will enjoy it as much as you might enjoy playing softball or golf. Of course, there are people who, for whatever reason, are *fanatics* about one particular sport and that is what they want to focus on. They watch the sport; they play the sport; they know all about the professionals and the history. If that's the case with you, wonderful. But on those rare occasions

57

when you cannot actually play or watch baseball, you might consider bowling or table tennis.

A third reason to try out different sports is that you might learn something from one sport that improves your performance in another. For example, in golf, a well-executed golf swing requires complete focus and determination paired with complete relaxation. Learning to do both together is not easy for most people. If you are like me, your "natural tendency" when you are "trying as hard as possible" is to tense your muscles, clench your jaw, and "make things happen." This will not work in golf. Actually, being able to focus while staying relaxed is *also* useful in many other sports where it is less obvious. For instance, a good tennis serve also requires relaxation and attention. But while this "relaxed attention" skill is useful in most sports, it is in golf where you will immediately get consistent feedback if you are tense. It is important to note that being relaxed does not mean you do not care. Of course, even the pro golfers feel nervous if they are in contention late Sunday (the last day of most golf tournaments). But they must learn to direct all that adrenaline and energy into the focus part and not into a tight body. You can learn this skill in golf but you can apply it to softball, tennis, basketball, and many other sports.

That is just one example. Surfing and gymnastics require excellent balance. But having good balance will serve you well in golf, in tennis, and most other sports as well. Table tennis requires fast reflexes. You have to see, anticipate and react to the ball very quickly. This comes in handy while playing the net in tennis, in handling bad bounces at shortstop and reacting quickly to opportunities on the basketball court.

In some cases, the benefits of one sport on another are more physical than skill-based. Backpacking for example, will strengthen your ankles and feet and improve your endurance. This can come in handy in long tennis matches or cross-country running. Generally speaking, engaging in multiple sports will provide you with better overall conditioning than any single sport. Some sports emphasize flexibility; some require strength; some require more speed; some require endurance. It is rare than any one sport requires *all* of these. If your main sport is golf, for example, you may want to supplement that with something that requires aerobic fitness such as running, swimming, soccer, tennis singles or basketball. If your main sport is body building, you may want to supplement that with yoga for balance and flexibility.

The fifth and final reason to enjoy more than one sport is simply opportunity. For most sports in most locations, you will not have access all day every day. Baseball may be rained out. The volleyball court may be booked. You might not be able to find a tennis partner. It may be too hot for long distance running. Golfing in a thunderstorm is a really silly way to commit suicide. So, when there is a thunderstorm, you can go bowling. If the volleyball court is unavailable, you can play table tennis in the basement. If it is too hot for long distance running outdoors, you can use the elliptical machine in the air conditioned gym. If you cannot play "real" golf outdoors, you may find a "virtual golf" place nearby. Any of these alternatives is healthier than watching television and *may* actually work to improve your main sport.

After all this, we still have not gotten to choosing your main sport! A lot depends on what we have already discussed. The *most* important factor is what you enjoy. Additional factors include the environment. If you are trying to decide between bowling and golf, where you live may make a difference. If you live in the southwestern US, you can play golf almost any day of the year. You won't if you live in Seattle or Minneapolis, although you can probably bowl in any major metro area in the USA. In some areas such as most of Canada and the Northeastern US, you can easily find a hockey game. This is less true in the hotter parts of the US. In some regions of the US, certain sports are very popular. Some states even have "official" sports. In Alaska, it is "mushing." If that's your thing, Hawaii would not be a good state for you. On the other hand, Hawaii's official sport is surfing. In Massachusetts, it is basketball (invented in Springfield, MA). In New Hampshire, it is skiing while in Texas, the official sport is Rodeo. None of these are particularly surprising, but unless you are willing and able to move to a state where your sport is popular, taking the the local possibilities for your sport into account seems wise.

There are physical factors that may have prevented you from becoming a *professional* athlete in a particular sport. For example, if you are 5'5" tall, you would have a hard time being a *professional* basketball player. Being short may also make it more difficult for you to outscore your opponents in amateur basketball, but if you enjoy basketball above all other sports, so what? If you enjoy a vast number of sports but don't have time to play them all, then you might take your talents into account in choosing what sports to focus on. If you tend to be very cool and relaxed under pressure, this could prove *especially* helpful in golf. If you are tall, this can used to your advantage in basketball, volleyball and tennis. If you have very fast reflexes, you might have find squash, table tennis, or racquetball to your liking. If you have good eye-hand coordination and are fairly large and strong, this can help with softball, baseball, or football.

Although these and other physical and mental constraints partly determine which sports are "best" for you, it is more important to understand what winning means to you. If you mostly want to participate in sports for the challenge and fun of it, then you want to choose the sports you most enjoy regardless of your physical and mental make up. On the other hand, if you really want to fill your bookcase with trophies then you will probably have to put much more focus on your natural talents in choosing your sport.

In addition to physical and geographical constraints, there may well be time constraints that influence your decision. One game of golf takes 3-5 hours. One game of table tennis takes a few minutes. Not only do different sports take different amounts of time; so too, different sports require different amounts of practice, training and money. Walking and running are free whereas polo, golf, and sailing are expensive. And, to complicate matters further, people differ in how much practice they need to stay at their peak. Some people can play golf or tennis once a month and do pretty well. I am not like that. I need to practice most sports a lot to come anywhere near my peak performance. So, in choosing your sports you will need to understand how much time and effort will be involved *for you* in reaching your goals. If you would like to be a scratch golfer but you only have five hours a week to devote to the game, you will *likely* not reach your goal till you retire.

In choosing your sport, do not ignore the social aspect. Giving proper weight to the social aspect depends on knowing how important that aspect is for you. If you do care, then you need to understand for your particular situation who you might be playing with. If your spouse wants to be a top triathlete for their age group and you want to play scratch golf you will be spending a lot less time together. And, maybe that is right for your relationship. Or, it may be that the local softball league irks you because no-one but you takes the game seriously. Everyone instead likes to drink a six pack during the game as well as after. Or, maybe everyone else in the league takes it much *too* seriously for your taste. Perhaps they feel it is worthwhile to break a few bones in order to score at home by running through the catcher but you might think this is only justified in the Major Leagues where people are paid a lot of money.

To repeat then, in choosing a sport you want to take into account several factors: what you enjoy; what talents you have; what makes sense for your location; what kind of time you are willing to put in; what the social situation is; and most importantly, what it means to *you* to be a winner.

CHAPTER TWELVE: CHOOSE YOUR VENUE.

Depending on your preferences, your abilities, your age, your sport and so on, particular venues are more or less advantageous to meeting your goals. The variations and combinations are nearly infinite but I will provide some examples. Then, you need to think through which venues will be most advantageous to you. As was the case in choosing your sport, the most important step is really understanding what winning means to you. To what extent are you in the game to stay young and healthy, to meet new people, to have fun with your friends, to improve your skills or to win games?

Understanding the answers to these questions is important for all your decisions, but for each sport, there are also subtleties that depend on you. For example, if you play golf, you may find it an interesting challenge to play with someone who consistently outdrives you. On the other hand, you might just find that frustrating and end up trying to hit the ball "with all your might" to "prove" you can hit the ball just as far. You might enjoy head to head competition and prefer match play rather than stroke play. You might find that you enjoy playing in a little rain while your opponents tend to fall apart. Or, you might find that very hot humid days wreak havoc with your game and you want to avoid them as much as possible. You might find that you play relatively well on courses with tight fairways and flat lies. Or, you might find that you enjoy the most or do your best when you play courses that are situated in beautiful surroundings —- or, you might find that distracting. Similarly, you might enjoy and do your best among people who like to talk a lot between shots during a round of golf. Or not. You might find that watching people with ungracious swings pains you. So, you may learn to look away or avoid playing with such people. You might find that you play your best and/ or enjoy early mornings or late afternoons. Perhaps you enjoy playing in windy conditions because of the extra challenge, or you might find that very frustrating. Maybe you only enjoy playing on courses that are very well maintained even if they are expensive. Perhaps you do not really care that much whether the fairways are perfect and the traps always raked. You really need to see what works for you. Of course, some of these preferences need not be fixed in stone. If you care to, you can change some of your attitudes and skills. You may at first "hate" courses with a lot of sand, but if you learn to hit out consistently to spots near the pins, you might change your mind. You might be more like me and happy to play golf under almost *any* circumstances.

Similarly, you may find certain kinds of tennis courts are better suited to your game. Concrete may be too fast or too hard on your legs. Clay courts may be too slow. Grass courts may be too hard to find. You might be very bothered by sun or wind and prefer to play indoors. You might find playing after dark under artificial light when it is cooler more to your liking. Or, you might find that for you, tracking the ball under these conditions is very difficult. You might enjoy playing against players who are "all business" and highly competitive. Or, maybe you find "friendlier" games suit your temperament. Personally, I enjoy playing in almost every situation.

You might find that you learn more and improve more when you are in a formal basketball league with regular games and referees. Or, maybe it is better for you to engage in pick-up games at the local playground. Perhaps you enjoy beach volleyball but not gym volleyball or vice versa. It all depends on what works for you. I would only caution against reaching a conclusion too quickly because of one or two good or bad experiences. Once you are actually playing *in* a particular venue, try to look at the advantages of that venue and see it as positively as possible. *After* you are done competing, reflect back on your experiences and think about whether this is the kind of venue you enjoy.

Part of the venue is not just the physical and social set-up but also the competitive nature of the situation. Depending on your goals and your abilities, you may want to compete at the highest level you can all the time. Or, you may want to compete against people in your own age group or ability level. You may like to compete against better players; they inspire and enliven you even if you seldom win. Or, you may find this extremely frustrating. Perhaps you enjoy a mix of these situations and sometimes compete against people

you can pretty much count on beating and
sometimes you play people who challenge you.

CHAPTER THIRTEEN: CHOOSE YOUR WEAPONS.

When I was a kid, I spent many hours playing baseball in a field near our house. We did not have anywhere near 18 kids so we played modified baseball. One day, when I was about twelve, one of our regular gang brought one of his uncle's golf balls and a golf club as well. The club was a driver made of real wood. We took turns hitting the ball and retrieving it. I had no idea how I was "supposed to" hit a golf ball. When my turn came, I remember staring at the beauty of the polished wood, dark and shiny with tiny sparkles from lighter grain within. I thought it would be pretty cool to hit anything with something so elegant. I swung and the ball started low and straight, rising into the air and completely disappearing into the distance. We knew there was no hope of finding the ball and thus the golf game ended. I am sure this wonderful drive was partly dumb luck and partly from not having any expectations or preconceptions but also partly because I was in love with that beautiful driver.

Almost every sport requires some kind of specialized clothing or equipment. Manufacturers of sports equipment will make all sorts of claims and many of them are even true. But the most important thing is for you to have confidence in whatever you are using and beyond that to really *love* it. If it is a set of golf clubs, you should love the feel and the look of the clubs and even the sound they make when you hit a shot crisply. Your clubs should feel like an extension of your body. If you play baseball, you need to *love* your mitt and your bat and the feel of the baseball in your hand. If you have a mitt, it's important that you "break it in" and if you have golf clubs, you should clean them yourself. The closer the relationship you can create between you and your equipment, the better. For this reason, I am not in favor of people constantly trying this club and that club, this tennis racquet and that one, this brand of mitt and that one. Find one that works and make it a part of you.

One way you can tell whether you have a relationship with your equipment is to notice how you feel about lending it to someone else. This should not be a casual thing. I am not saying never lend someone your equipment, but it should make you feel queasy. It should feel more like having them date your daughter than like letting them borrow your lawnmower.

To take another analogy, our immune systems work by recognizing what is "us" and what is "not us." This is generally good because it helps us fight off infections. But it also makes transplants difficult. The body recognizes the foreign organ as "not self" and tries to kill it off. Generally, doctors must give immune suppressing drugs to transplant recipients so that the organ is not "rejected." But when it comes to sports equipment, you have more conscious control over your attitude. You can *will* yourself to view an excellent piece of equipment as part of you. If you do, your

69

performance will be considerably better than if you are constantly questioning whether this is right for you or complaining that it doesn't feel right or is uncomfortable.

A few years ago, Serena Williams was playing in the semi-finals of a *major* tennis tournament and the wind kept blowing her skirt around and bothering her. When she was serving for instance, she kept bouncing the ball and then just as she was about to toss it, she needed to re-adjust her skirt. (I realize that it can be tricky to serve with gusty winds, but this was over and above that — another distraction). Seriously? How could a major player and her team not have provided her with clothing she was comfortable in? She went on to lose the match and I am convinced that her lack of confidence and comfort with her outfit was part of the problem.

Loving the things that connect you to your work applies far beyond sports equipment, of course. It applies to machinery, software, people, methods, and so on. If you are making bread, you are not going to do a stellar job unless you love bread. If you are doing delicate surgery, you need to feel the instruments are extensions of your hands. If you are a manager, you need to appreciate and trust your employees. If you are growing tomatoes, you need to really love those tomatoes for best results. And, if you want to be able to pull off that shoestring catch in center field, it really helps if you love that glove.

CHAPTER FOURTEEN: CHOOSE YOUR OPPONENTS.

As is the case with most decisions, you need to understand what winning means to you in order to do a good job of choosing your opponents. Obviously, you don't always have complete freedom in who your opponents are. If you enter a tournament or a league, your opponents may be chosen for you by the organizers. But on many occasions you do have some control over who you play against. If your goal is to win as many times as possible, then you can choose easy opponents. If your goal is to improve your game, then you may want to play against more difficult opponents. The impact of your opponent on your own game will depend on the sport. For example, if you are playing golf, your opponent's play should not really affect yours very much. There are exceptions of course. If your opponent is extremely slow, it may affect your play although this will be mainly influenced by whether you *let* it influence you. I have played with people whose swing I find painful to watch. So I don't watch. In tennis, on the other hand, the opponents skill will directly impact your own practice during games. If you play against someone who is somewhat better, it will tend to enhance your skills but only up to a point. If you play with someone who aces you every time, what do you really learn?

As a general rule, it probably works best for most sports to choose opponents who are approximately at the same level as you or slightly better. This will include some who will mainly beat you and some whom you will mainly beat. This will typically do the most to improve your game. However, if you are mainly enjoying sports for the social aspect, then you may want to mainly play with a particular group or team. If you are mainly playing for the exercise, you may want to play mainly with people who maximize that exercise. For instance, if you like to walk and carry your clubs when you play golf, you will want to join foursomes who do the same. If you are playing tennis, you may want to find opponents who run you from side to side and use drop shots and lobs rather than someone who tries to hit outright winners. In the latter case, the rallies are likely to be very short.

You might be even more specific in your choice of opponents in some sports. For example, if you want to improve your return of serve in tennis, then clearly it is advantageous to have an opponent who serves well. It is probably useful to have a variety of opponents with excellent flat serves, slice serves and topspin serves. On the other hand, if you want to improve your putting in golf, it doesn't make much difference who else is in your foursome provided you don't choose someone who talks during your putting or stands in your line[25].

---

[25] In golf, your "line" is an imaginary line from your ball to the hole but extending beyond the hole and behind your ball as well. It is considered bad form to stand in someone else's line while they are putting or to walk on it before.

In some sports, such as tennis, it is useful to spend some time playing with an opponent who is willing and able to do drills with you as well as play regulation games. For instance, if you want to work on your backhand after having a series of lessons on that shot, it is very helpful to have a practice partner who will hit most shots to your backhand. You might want to work on your return of serve and pair up with someone who wants to work on their serve. In team sports such as soccer, baseball, and football, the game play is typically too complicated to do this with "opponents" and targeted drills are carried out with your teammates. Regardless of your sport or how you want to choose your opponents, remember that without opponents there is no sport. For that reason, treat your opponents with respect. They are the file that sharpens your blade and you are the file that sharpens theirs.

CHAPTER FIFTEEN: CHOOSE YOUR
COACHES: THE GOOD, THE BAD, AND THE
UGLY.

Trainers and coaches can be an awesome aid in
reaching your goals for any sport. A good coach
helps you stay focussed, diagnoses what is
happening, watches you and determines what is
wrong and helps you fix it. A good coach helps you
choose appropriate goals, venues, and opponents.
Unfortunately, not every coach you run into will
necessarily be a good coach for you at this
particular time. Being a good coach is different
from being a good athlete or being good or even
great at a particular sport.

A good coach for one person may not be a good
coach for another person. Some coaches will
stress the mechanics of a good tennis stroke,
batting cut, or golf swing. If your mechanics are
bad *and* you can learn mechanics from being
corrected, this *may* help you. But other coaches
may stress more the *feel* of a good tennis stroke,
batting cut or golf swing and this may help you a
lot more than being "reset" into the correct
positions over and over. Still other coaches may
use visualization or exercises or special
equipment to help you. Some of these various
techniques will resonate with some players and
leave others completely cold. You have to see
what kind of coaching really works for you.

Just as it is important for you to understand your
goals and what winning means to you, so too it is

vital for your coach to understand what you are after in a sport. Maybe you are a golfer whose current handicap[26] is 20 and you want to be a scratch golfer. If you share this with your potential coach they may say, "Come on! Get serious! You're fifty years old. Let's pick a more realistic goal like a 15 handicap." Then, you may well want to get a different coach. Do not get me wrong. If you really want to improve that much, it *will* likely be a lot of work. But you need to believe in yourself and you need a coach who believes in you as well.

Or, no coach at all.

There *have* been excellent athletes who are self-taught like the golfer Bubba Watson. Would he have been better with a coach? We will never know for sure, but it seems unlikely. The vast majority of folks, however, will do much better with a good coach, but may well do worse with a really bad coach. How can you tell the difference? You probably need to try the person out and see how you feel. Trust your gut. Do you feel like this coach is improving your performance? You have to make an honest assessment of how teachable you are as well. If your coach suggests changing your grip

---

[26] Roughly speaking, the difference between getting all pars on a course and what you get is your "handicap." Since golf courses are 18 holes, a 20 handicap means you are taking about one extra shot on every hole. A 20 handicap is slightly worse than the average recreational male golfer while a 15 is slightly better.

in tennis, batting, golf, table tennis, or squash and you *immediately* reject the idea because it feels "unnatural" maybe this is not going to work, not because the coach is bad per se, but is not going to synch up with your way of learning.

Some signs of a coach that is not likely to work for you include the following.

1. Jumping to conclusions. If a pro watches you hit one or two strokes or two drives or take two jump shots or whatever and then starts trying to change your grip, your stance, your swing path etc., they are probably not going to work very well for you. They do not have enough evidence yet to know whether this is even your typical result. You may be doing something different because of nerves or you are trying to swing the way you know it "should be done" even though in a real game, you hardly ever do this. A good coach should let your warm up first and then watch a fair number of performances before drawing any conclusions about possible errors.

2. Ruining your self-confidence. "You are using your hands too much. You are likely to hook[27] the ball out of bounds[28] like that. We need to start over." Maybe you very seldom, in fact, hook the (golf) ball out of bounds. But now the seed is planted in your head. It might well be that a shot with a lot of hand action works quite well for you. Different people are different and there are *many* good golf swings with different degrees of leg, hip, shoulder, arm, and hand involvement.

3. Micromanaging after every shot. If your coach tells you what you did wrong after every shot, this is probably a bad sign. "That time, you didn't bend your knees enough. That time, you didn't bring your racquet back far enough. That time, you forgot to follow through." The coach might even be correct. But this kind of detailed feedback after

---

[27] In golf, (for a right handed player), if you put a lot of right to left (counter-clockwise) spin on the ball it will curve to the left. This is called a hook. If you hit the ball with lot of left to right (clockwise) spin it will curve to the right. This is called a slice. Putting a little counter-clockwise spin on and making it curve only a little to the left is called a draw. Putting only a little clockwise spin on and making it cure a little to the right is called a fade. In some cases, players make the ball curve on purpose in order to go around an obstruction.

[28] In golf, if you hit your ball "out of bounds", you must go back and hit the shot again. You have to count both shots *and* a penalty stroke. So, if you hit your first shot out of bounds, now you have to re-hit that first shot and you are deemed to have hit *three* strokes already.

each shot will cause you to over-think what is going on and ruin any kind of flow with your shots.

If professional coaches occasionally do this, dads and husbands are experts at this kind of bad advice. I have had the misfortune, as have most golfers, of witnessing a husband attempt to micromanage their wife's golf swing this way. Yikes! This is unpleasant for everyone in the foursome (except, apparently, the self-appointed expert) but cannot fail to make the wife's swing worse and ruin her enjoyment of the game. I suppose that might possibly be the point of this kind of "instruction" but I suspect it is more likely a desire to help and a complete lack of understanding about how to do it effectively. Theoretically, one could imagine an excellent female golfer doing this to their novice husband, but I have never actually seen such a thing in real life.

CHAPTER SIXTEEN: YOU MAY FIND THIS
GRAIN OF SALT USEFUL.

One of the best-selling sports books of all time is
Harvey Penick's Little Red Book: Lessons and
Teaching from a Lifetime in Golf. Many of the
lessons in the book are applicable to other sports
as well. In the book, he describes one case where
he gave a student some advice on changing their
grip on the club. When the student came back
later, they complained that they were hooking
everything now. When Harvey looked at the
student's grip, he saw that he had greatly
exaggerated the advice that Harvey had given.
Harvey summarized it that he had asked the
student to take an aspirin and instead, they had
swallowed the whole bottle.

Any piece of good advice can be turned into bad
advice by taking it too far to the extreme. For
instance, I claim that increasing your flexibility,
strength, and endurance will tend to improve your
performance at any sport. But take *any* advice with
"a grain of salt." If you bowl six days a week and
your average is 220, and now you begin on such
an extensive fitness program that you drop fifty
pounds and only have time to bowl once a week, it
is likely that your average will go down. (You might
live longer, by the way). But that lack of practice is
most likely going to harm your average more than
the increased conditioning will improve your
bowling.

I am trying to give the best advice I can in a book without meeting you, without knowing your age, your goals and so on. To make the book "work" for you, you will have to apply some common sense and some creative thinking to see how it can be used as a tool for you to reach your goals in your sport given your body.

CHAPTER SEVENTEEN: PREPARE YOUR BODY.

So the old saw goes about golf: "Golf is 80 per cent mental and 80 per cent physical." Pretty much the same can be said about any other sport. In order to play well, you need to have the mental game *and* the physical game in good shape. In this chapter, we focus on preparing your body. Doing this optimally is slightly different for different sports, but first let us focus on ways to prepare your body that are good for any sport.

It is good to follow the "rules" of health at any age but following rules of health is more and more important as you get older. You might "get away with" eating junk food when you are fifteen and still play well or do well at track but if you keep that up all your life, you will not play well in your sixties and beyond (if you even live that long). Similarly, when you are young, you may not die of a heart attack from smoking or get lung cancer or emphysema but even when young you will decrease your performance. The cumulative effects, of course, are well known.

Some people protest that the "rules" of health keep changing (so therefore do whatever you like). It is true that there have been some changes in nutritional guidelines over the years. However, experts have always advised (at least in my lifetime) to eat a variety of foods, that vegetables are good for you, that refined sugar is bad for you and that junk food is not food. Being overweight will not help you in the vast majority of sports. It may help in sumo wrestling. Being overweight will definitely not help you stay healthy. And it will not help in sports that requires speed and agility. Health experts have also advised throughout my lifetime that fresh air and exercise are good for you. More recently, we have documented benefits of plenty of exercise that extend well beyond good cardiovascular health to include keeping your brain working better, keeping your *mood* better, and reducing the risk of osteoporosis and some types of cancer. Studies have also more recently discovered that you should not only exercise regularly but you should *also* avoid prolonged periods of sitting without a break. Now, we also know that positive social interaction is good for your health! And, although some cultures have known for a long while that meditation is good for you, western medicine has now confirmed the benefits.

So, rather than making it sound as though the rules of good health keep changing willy-nilly, I think it would be more accurate to say that we now have a more detailed view of the rules of health than we had a hundred years ago. In most cases, the things like exercise that were *always* known to be good are *still* known to be good but now we have even more detailed evidence of the benefits. Needless to say, huge changes in lifestyle should be undertaken slowly and you should discuss them with your doctor. Just because exercise is a good thing does not mean if you've been sedentary for the last 35 years you should jump up off the couch and run a marathon. Similarly, if you are obese, the healthiest way to lose weight is still gradually and steadily. Discuss these things with your doctor.

Ultimately, a well rounded exercise program should ideally include 3-4 days a week of strength training, 5-6 days a week of cardio conditioning, and 6-7 days a week of stretching. I say "ultimately" because this is something to work up to if you are currently sedentary. I say "ideally" because such a program takes a lot of time. In addition to improving your performance at virtually every sport, an exercise program may well help you live a longer, happier, healthier, more productive life. You will *look* more attractive as well. An additional benefit of exercise is that it will lower your chances of having a minor or major injury. All in all, there are few investments with a higher ROI than exercise. Realistically, some people are extremely busy and finding the time to exercise optimally may be difficult. I am planning another book that deals specifically with this challenge. Meanwhile, please keep in mind that major illnesses, injuries, and death may put more of a crimp in your lifestyle than an hour a day of exercise.

While a well-rounded exercise program is foundational to doing well in a sport, you may also want to add specific exercises or drills aimed at your particular sport or sports. For example, if you want to do the best you can at tennis or golf, the forearm muscles are important. Many people find wrist curls, or squeezing a ball useful for these sports. If you play full length tennis singles matches, you will want to be in very good cardio shape. Of course, that can be of some benefit to any sport, but the relative rewards will be greater in basketball, soccer, or tennis than they will in golf, softball, or volleyball.

Good nutrition is likewise valuable in any sport, but this will be particularly true in sports that really push you physically such as triathlons, cycling, track, swimming, or basketball. A varied diet that is mainly composed of "real" food rather than processed junk filled with sugar, fat, and salt to make it seem tasty will most likely meet all your nutritional needs. Typically your doctor will ask for blood tests at your annual physical that will reveal any glaring problems such as iron deficiency or diabetes. Limiting refined sugar and starches and including enough fiber in your diet have been increasingly found to be important in recent years. There are a huge number of different philosophies and diets on the market and perhaps you will find one that works particularly well for you. However, do not let the diversity of opinions on, say, the value of meat in your diet, become an excuse for not following what nearly everyone agrees on which is to avoid the crap food. Crap food is often packaged in brightly colored containers. This is to trick your brain into thinking you are eating some colorful berries, fruits, or vegetables that are filled with important phyto-chemicals.

In the stone age, it was often difficult for people to find enough sugar, salt, and fat to survive. So our brains are wired to like these things. Sure enough, crap food is often laced with extra salt, sugar, and/or fat to again fool your brain into thinking you have eaten something nutritious. Crap food is also advertised to make you think that eating crap food and/or providing it to your family will make you a loved and loving person; that it will make you sexy or adventurous; that it is something "smart" to do or that all kinds of fun things will happen to you. Notice that blueberries and apples and oranges and kale and walnuts are not advertised with these kinds of messages. They don't need to be because they actually do provide nutrition.

Another important way to prepare you body is to get enough sleep. If, for any reason, you are not generally getting at least 7 hours sleep a night, that is going to hinder your athletic performance. Of course, many people get nervous before a big competition and may have trouble falling asleep. I wouldn't worry about missing some sleep on any particular night. (But I will give some suggestions about not over-stressing about a competition later). If you are constantly having trouble going to sleep, it may be worth some analysis of your habits. For some people, any caffeine after noontime makes it hard to fall asleep. Watching the news right before bed — news which is typically concerned with terrible and violent things that are beyond your control to do anything about —- is probably not a good idea. If you fall asleep but then wake up and cannot get back to sleep easily, this might be because of drinking too much alcohol before bed.

Of course, when it comes to "preparing your body" using illegal drugs is not a good idea. You might find that a little alcohol is okay for you. But if you are using it *during* athletic performances because it helps you relax, find better and more permanent ways to handle your nervousness. Illegal performance enhancing drugs are a hugely bad idea. Many professional athletes have taken the risk of the significant side-effects because they feel it will make them millionaires and/or they will not get caught. Of course, as a "weekend warrior" you will probably not be subject to the kind of drug tests that professional athletes are. But if you win *and* you were using an illegal drug, will that really help you meet your goals? You will never know whether you won *because* you cheated. Even if no-one else every finds out, you will know. Perhaps equally importantly, your body will know. Is it really worth cancer or going into a rage and killing someone so you can hit the softball a few feet farther? You'd be far better off spending your money on lessons.

CHAPTER EIGHTEEN: PREPARE YOUR ATTITUDE.

There is not just one "correct" attitude. To some extent, the best attitude depends on your general disposition and on the sport. The amount of intense physical drive and how that is distributed over time differs somewhat from sport to sport. In golf, for example, you need to have mental focus while being physically relaxed. In many sports, the type of mental focus shifts over time. For example, in golf, you can "think about" where you want your approach shot to land and what type of approach shot as you walk up the fairway after your drive. In tennis, as you retrieve the ball before your serve, you have a chance to think about where and how you want to serve. Once "play" starts in any sport, you do not want to think much about mechanics and probably don't have time to do much thinking about strategy and tactics until the next break in the action. Each sport suggests its own rhythm of thinking and doing.

Many of the mental attitudes you want to prepare, however, are good ones in *any sport, and for that matter in any life endeavor.* We might summarize these as: Learning, Staying in the Moment, Positivity, Acceptance, and Love. Let us next examine what is meant by each of these mental attitudes or stances and then look into how to achieve them.

Having a learning attitude means that regardless of what happens, you need to remember that it offers the possibility of a learning experience. This "learning" occurs at many levels. For instance, if you are way behind and come back to win, you can "learn" to never count yourself out. If you hit a particular shot particularly badly, instead of berating yourself, you may contemplate what happened and how to fix it, within limits. During a match or game is not the best time to experiment with new technique. But if you know you have a tendency to stop trying to move into position too early and you recognize that this happened on the last shot, you can remind yourself to be sure to get into position.

You want to do this reminding however, before the point starts, not during the point. Because during "play" you want to stay in the moment. You do not want to worry about what the score might be later or what mistakes you made a few moments ago. You want to train your mind to focus on the now. Doing so bestows a threefold benefit. First, by focusing on the now, you maximize your chances of doing well right this moment. Second, by focusing, you allow your brain to learn more effectively. Third, by staying in the moment, you will avoid emotional extremes that can wreak havoc with your game.

Positivity means always believing that you can win or do well or learn. I believe this attitude goes best with staying in the moment. If you are a swimming against someone who is consistently faster and has won every race, it is probably not productive to try to convince yourself that you are already a better swimmer. You can, however, reasonably believe that you could win on this particular day. Similarly, if you are a golfer with a 20 handicap playing straight up against someone who is a scratch golfer, it is probably not going to work to convince yourself that you will win the match. *However,* it is perfectly reasonable to think you can hit a better approach shot *right now* or one putt this green. If you are a 3.0 tennis player and playing against a 4.0 player, focus on returning *this serve* and doing it with a positive expectation that you can reach the ball and put it back deep. And, who knows? From all these small battles won, you may also win the war.

Acceptance means to accept whatever is actually true about reality right now. Maybe you just hit a marvelous tee shot down the middle of the fairway and you landed in a deep divot. Your opponent on the other hand, may have hooked his ball wildly into the woods…and had the ball bounce back out onto the fairway thirty yards ahead of yours! Is that "fair"? Of course not. But I can guarantee you that it happens. If you could, you might rewrite history. But you cannot. So acceptance means to focus on hitting the best shot you can under the actual circumstances of play. Sometimes a puff of wind blows unfavorably to you. Sometimes the ref or ump makes a bad call. Sometimes, a less skillful opponent enjoys all the luck in the world. All of that happens. The question is, what can you do in response? One option is to focus on how unfair it all is and make yourself upset. That will maximize the negative impact on your game. Or, you can accept reality as it actually is, laugh at the vagaries of life and make the best of it. That will minimize any potentially negative impact and may even have a positive influence.

Finally, what on earth would we be doing talking about "love" in a sports book? I already mentioned that it helps to love your equipment. So too, it helps to love the conditions, whatever they are. Is there an unpredictable wind blowing? Cool! What an interesting challenge! How can I use these unique circumstances to my advantage? Is it raining? Nice! It feels great to be alive! How can I use this to my advantage? Are the golf greens exceptionally fast? Right! My kind of greens! Are they ridiculously slow? Awesome! My kind of greens! Is it exceptionally hot out? Wonderful! Because I am in great shape and know enough to stay hydrated so this is a definite advantage to me! Is there a lot of noise from other competitors, traffic, planes? Good! Because I have great concentration skills and my opponents are going to be a lot more distracted than I am. Is the crowd with me? Great! I can build on their energy and use it to my advantage! Is the crowd against me? Great! I can build on their energy and use it to my advantage!

Of course, the preceding advice presumes that you do not have supernatural powers. If you *do* have supernatural powers, then by all means *use* those supernatural powers to change the wind, the sun, the rain, the surface of the courts, the speed of the greens, your opponent's annoying habits, or the tenor of the crowd. Be my guest. If, however, you were born *without* supernatural powers, then whining is not likely to change any of these external conditions. In that case, embracing them and working with them will work better.

Needless to say, you want to love not only the particular conditions, but the sport itself. Love the constraints, the rules, the traditions, the formats, the competitions. Know your sport inside and out. Love knowing the little nuances. Granted, some sports, like golf are perhaps particularly conducive to a love-hate relationship rather than a love relationship. Nonetheless, focus as best you can on the love part. And that love should extend, in some way, even to your competitors. Without your competitors, the sport would not really exist so you should be glad for them and glad they are skillful enough to test you. You don't want to love them so much that you prefer they *win,* but you do want them to give you a good match.

So, you may say, it is all well and good but how do I actually achieve these aspects of a positive mental attitude? The first and most important thing to realize is that it takes practice. For most people, changing from a demanding and whining attitude to a healthy and positive one will not come instantaneously. You need to *practice* having a good mental attitude. You can anticipate this as you prepare mentally for a match in the same way that you visualize your play. You can anticipate yourself being positive and taking a learning attitude, for example.When you describe your experience afterwards, be sure to take a positive approach then too. Whether you won or lost, say something positive about both yourself and your opponent. (Here is one place where the winning weekend warrior really can emulate the best professional athletes). Remember too that you are incredibly lucky to be healthy enough, wealthy enough, and to have the time to participate in a sport. Having these positive mental attitudes will help increase your chances of winning and meeting your goals whatever they are. It will also help you stay healthy and it will make you a desirable participant so that others will seek you out to play. I recommend the books of Bob Rotella for further help in this area.

CHAPTER NINETEEN: PREPARE YOUR SKILL.

"Prepare your skill" seems like an odd phrase. Why didn't I just say "practice"? I use the term "prepare your skill" because practice does not necessarily lead to improved performance. Only *proper* practice improves your skill. And only *strategic* proper practice will result in your achieving your goals. Let us take a few examples.

If you are swimming improperly, then putting more and more laps in at the pool will increase your endurance and burn calories. So, there are some benefits. However, it will not improve your performance nearly so much as practicing a better technique. If you are out on the driving range hooking 300 balls a day, that is not going to improve your golf game any more than hooking 100 balls a day. In both cases, the result will pretty much be zero. If you have a tennis backhand that consists of poking the ball back, practicing that bad stroke for an hour a day will not do very much to improve your winning percentage. It might make you a little more consistent in this case and improve your percentage a little, but not much. It would be better to learn a powerful one handed or two handed backhand and then practice that stroke. Of course, if you are only playing tennis to burn calories, and you really don't care about winning matches, then it might make more sense to run around every backhand. This will definitely force you to burn more calories.

In general, if part of your goal is to win more or to improve your skills, then you need to get some instruction, experiment yourself, watch pros, or read books in order to see how to improve some aspect of your game and then practice that improvement until it becomes natural and reliable. Practicing the *proper* technique (or *a* proper technique since there is often more than one) will cause improvement over time. Strategic practice means that you (perhaps with the help of a coach) determine which aspects of your game are the most valuable to practice. For instance, if you are already a scratch golfer but cannot hit a reliable flop shot, you may want to learn to do just that. This shot allows you to hit a high soft shot over an obstacle and land the ball near the pin. However, if you are a thirty handicapper hitting one out of five fairways, then putting a lot of time into learning a flop shot is not strategic. Perfecting the flop shot might save you one stroke a round, but hitting three out of five fairways will save you a lot more strokes.

Similarly, if you are a baseball pitcher, it may well be worth putting in the time to improve your batting average from .100 to .200. But it is probably not worth putting in the time trying to raise your batting average from .300 to .400. You would be better off honing your pitching skills. If you are a tennis player and right now are forty pounds overweight and have a weak serve, it is probably not worth spending a lot of time learning to serve and volley. You are not going to win more points by serving and then "rushing" up halfway to the service line where any decent return will have to played off your shoestrings. If you do manage to volley from that position and continue to the net, then if you happen to be facing an opponent who is capable of thought, they will lob the next shot back to the baseline. Again, you need to know your goals. If your only goal is to get a heart attack so your spouse can get the insurance money, this might be a good way to spend your time. But if your goal is to improve your winning percentage, not so much. First, lose the forty pounds and improve your serve. *Then*, revisit the issue of whether it is worth it to rush the net.

Deciding how much to practice which aspects of the sport is not a simple problem to solve. For instance, many books on golf point out that you are probably going to hit your driver fourteen times on a round and you will hit your putter more like thirty-six times. "Drive for show; putt for dough" is a common refrain. So, does this mean you should spend 2.5 X as much on putting practice as on driving practice? Not necessarily. It depends on how much these bad shots cost you and also on how much practice improves your skill. For instance, if you are playing narrow courses and hooking fifty per cent of your tee shots out of bounds, these bad tee shots are costing a *lot* of strokes per round. If you are leaving a lot of putts a foot from the hole, those misses are costing you one stroke each. You may find that four hours practice per week on driving accuracy improves your accuracy from 50 per cent to 75 per cent and that most of your fairway misses are now in the rough, not out of bounds. This will lower your score considerably; perhaps by 8-10 strokes. You might find that practicing putting for four hours a week improves your average putts per round from 38 putts to 36 putts thus saving two strokes.

Of course, if you are a twenty-five handicapper, you could just quit your day job and devote 14 hours a day to practicing golf. This would allow you to practice driving *and* putting and chipping and pitching and sand shots and flop shots and bump and run and sidehill lies and uphill lies and downhill lies and hitting out of a divot and putting from off the green, and hitting out of deep rough. In this way, your game would improve *much* more than practicing four hours a week, at least until the finance company repossess your home, your car and your golf clubs. Realistically, most people cannot practice their sport fourteen hours a *week* let alone fourteen hours a day. So, it does become very important to use the time that is available wisely; that is, strategically.

A really good coach can be very helpful in determining how best to use your time. But it also depends on you — understanding your goals and also what kinds of practice you enjoy. If spending four hours a week on the putting green would improve your game more than four hours on the driving range, *but* you love going to driving range but practicing on the putting green makes you think of changing your sport to sky diving without a parachute, then it makes more sense to go to the driving range. Being dead reduces your chances of winning in almost any sport to near zero.

If you do not have a coach, you will have to be your own coach, which is probably better than being your own lawyer, but not by a lot. Still, there are successful trainer-less athletes, so here are some things to consider when thinking strategically about what to practice and how to practice. First, what facilities are available or could be made available to you? Your tennis serve can be practiced alone with a bucket of balls on any empty tennis court. Practicing *return of serve* requires a partner. Driving ranges for golf are much more widely available than good short game practice facilities. You can easily find a spot to practice your basketball foul shots and your dribbling but practicing ball stealing and shot blocking will require others to cooperate. Running and cycling can be practiced almost anywhere. Practicing your softball pitching can be done against a brick wall while hitting will require a batting cage or a cooperative partner. Practicing the discus obviously requires a discus. Practicing the discus more than once will require a bunch of them and a large field. Etc. You get the idea.

Besides facilities, it is important to understand your "edge." You definitely want to practice that. You also want to determine what kind of practice would do the most to help you achieve your goals. This will depend on how often a particular skill is or could be demanded by the situations as well how much practice will help. In some cases, you may want to practice something that is synergistic with your edge. For example, your tennis game may include a great top-spin lob. But if your opponent spends all their time at the baseline, the effectiveness of the lob is less than it might be. If you can also learn a great drop shot, you can draw your opponent in (or win the point outright) and then follow up with a great lob. In baseball or softball, you may be a great singles hitter. If you can reliably learn to steal second as well, then you will tend to score a lot more runs.

By way of contrast, there are many skills that "theoretically" could come in handy but unless you have infinite time, they are not worth practicing. For instance, you may have a really good two-handed backhand. Of all the things you could practice to improve your tennis game, *also* learning a good one handed backhand is low on the priority list. Why bother? In golf, there are occasions when it is useful to hit the "driver off the deck" but they are rare. If you are keen to learn it because it is fun, go for it. But don't expect such a shot to improve your score or your winning percentage much. In basketball, you *could* practice a mid court jump shot for hours just in case you happen to be there with a half second left to play. Maybe this will increase your chances of making such a shot and being a hero from one in a thousand to three in a thousand. But practicing foul shots, three pointers, passes, and layups will do more to improve your team's chances of winning. In baseball, if you play the infield, it is definitely worth practicing handling grounders. Your team should also practice turning double plays. It is probably *not* worthwhile to practice triple plays however. The occasions are rare and the skills needed are already going to arise from practicing double plays. Similarly, it is worth a little team practice on a run-down for a player caught between two bases. It is probably not worthwhile to practice running players down with the bases loaded, at least not for weekend warriors. Just keep the lead runner from scoring!

Regardless of what skill or skills you decide to focus on, it helps to have some sort of metrics of your success. If you are practicing chipping in golf, for example, keep track of how many chips are within three and six feet of the hole out of twenty. See whether this is improving over time. If it isn't, you need to change your technique or practice something that will improve. If you are practicing overhead smashes and lobs for tennis, play against a partner and keep track of points. First, one person lobs and the other smashes for ten then switch. Here, it may not be so obvious to measure improvement because you might (hopefully) both be improving at the same time.

Be alert for the possibility that improving your skill may mean that you can or should change your strategy as well. If you play tennis doubles and are terrible at the net, you may want to play back on your partner's second serve and possibly even the first serve. As you get more and more capable at the net, however, you will want to play up more often. Eventually, if you are physically capable, you may want to follow your own serve to the net as well. Similarly, if your golf approach shots become more accurate and reliable, you can try to land the ball closer to the pin rather than the middle of the green. In basketball, if you greatly increase the accuracy of your three point shots, you may not need to try to drive in so often. If you increase your lacrosse passing accuracy, there is less need for longer riskier shots.

CHAPTER TWENTY: PRACTICE IN CONTEXT.

If you have played much golf, you have probably been part of a foursome where one of your playing partners slices the ball into the woods off the tee. They re-tee and hook the next ball out of bounds. Then, they say, "I can't understand it. I go to the driving range and hit them straight as an arrow!" Well, I *do* understand it! It makes perfect sense. Here's why. When someone goes to the driving range and hits drive after drive, they are probably in a completely different frame of mind than when they are actually playing a round of golf. They are not worried about hitting a bad shot. They are not worried about letting their partner down. So, mentally, the context is completely different. But, it isn't just the mental context that is different.

If you go to the driving range and hit a tee shot with your driver and then hit another and another and another, your *muscles* are in a completely different state that they are when you are playing a round of golf. The muscles and joints needed to hit a tee shot are completely warmed up and relaxed because you are doing it over and over with very little pause. In a typical practice session at the driving range, most golfers are hitting there tee shots with 20 to 45 seconds between tee shots. In a round of golf, it is 15 to 45 *minutes* between tee shots with the driver. So, not only are you in a different frame of mind, your body is in a different state as well. This is particularly true if you are playing cart golf and you drove from green to tee. Your body is much less "warmed up" than when you are continuously hitting tee shots on the driving range.

But wait. It gets worse. When you hit your thirtieth tee shot on the driving range, you have probably just hit twenty nine tee shots in a row right before that tee shot! When you are playing golf, you have (hopefully) just hit zero tee shots in a row before that one. You have probably hit at least one iron shot and a couple of putts with your putter. If you are a professional golfer and you've put in a billion hours of practice, it still makes some difference but not a lot. If, on the other hand, you really are a weekend warrior and you only practice golf five to ten hours a week, then you are much more in the groove on the driving range than you are during a round. So, it is a *triple* whammy! A "perfect storm."

Oh, hold on. I almost forgot! If you are on the driving range, you are facing a wide open space! On most golf courses, when you step up to hit your tee shot, there is trouble on the left *and* on the right. There are many visible obstacles such as out of bounds, houses, trees, sand, and water! So, the apparent task of hitting a "good" drive seems much more difficult than on the driving range. Even if you are "talented enough" to slice or hook the ball *completely off the range,* there is no real penalty! You already paid for your bucket of balls. The manager does not run out onto the astroturf and demand you pay for a lost ball.

Does this mean that it is pointless to practice tee shots on the driving range? Of course not! But it does mean that you should try to make *most* of your practice on the driving range as close as possible to what you face on a real golf course. You cannot duplicate everything about playing a real round of golf, but you can duplicate a lot! Most of your practice should be based on playing a real course. That is, after you have stretched and warmed up a bit, you should imagine playing a real round of golf on a real course. You imagine what hole number one is and think about what club you need to hit. Driver? Okay. Then hit driver. Where is the spot you want to hit this? Is it vital to hit a long drive? Is it important to favor the left side? Now, choose points on the driving range within which that tee shot needs to land. Now, pick out a very small and specific target within that range. Use that as your aiming point. Now, you hit the shot and assess how it went. Did you get close to your aiming point? Did you get within the range of good shots? How far out from the green are you? Use that estimate to determine the next club you need. Then practice that iron shot. Did you hit the imaginary green? Now take out your putter and imagine hitting some putts and swing the putter, making sure you are using a good putting stroke. Imagine them as being good putts. Now, think about the second hole. This is how *most* of your practice should be.

Should you *ever* just hit a series of balls with your driver or seven iron? Of course. If you are taking a lesson, or you are trying to learn how to hit your driver, it might pay to spend some concentrated time "making sure" you are grooving your new skill. But, as I say, most of your practice should be as "in context" as possible.

This approach applies to other sports as well. If you want to train for a triathlon for instance, it helps a lot to do some "brick training" where you do a swim followed by a bike ride or a bike ride followed by a run. You need to train your body for the transitions between events as well as the separate events. Most of your swimming training will be in situations where there is not so much chaos as in a triathlon, but you do want to be prepared, at least mentally, for being hit and kicked during the race. If you have to practice long swims only in a pool, make sure you don't grab the end of the pool at every lap. You want to be used to swimming in open water.

If you are training for basketball, it is fine to spend some time dribbling, foul shooting and practicing lay-ups and jump shots. But it is better practice to spend most of that practice with a buddy playing for points and at least putting up some defense so you get the feel of doing all these things under pressure and with someone trying to prevent you from executing the shot.

Let's say you are training for tennis doubles with your partner. You want to practice serve and return of serve. Don't just return the serve anywhere. Make a point to return most serves deep to the server's corner (and away from an imaginary net player). If you know you are going to be playing against a poacher, you want to practice some down the line returns as well as some deep lobs.

Let's say your are in a team practice for baseball or softball and someone is hitting fly balls to the outfield. Okay, but there should be an imagined base runner situation as well and the outfielders should know that situation and how to respond to it if they catch the ball or it drops in for a hit. The outfielders should also practice calling balls that are hit between them and saying "back" or "in" for balls hit directly to another outfielder. (It is more obvious to the left fielder whether a ball hit directly in line with the center fielder is going to drop in front of the center fielder or go over their head).

There is a place for practicing isolated skills of course, but generally, people would do much better to practice in context much more than they do. Keep this in mind when designing your own program of practice.

CHAPTER TWENTY-ONE: FOCUS ON WHAT COUNTS.

I will repeat the mantra that in order to make the most of this chapter you really have to understand what winning means to you. If the main pleasure you get in tennis, for instance, is to hit an ace every twenty serves or so, then by all means, be my guest however it impacts the score, and hit every serve full speed. If you want to win more matches, however, you would be better off by varying the speed and placement and spin of your serves and getting a high percentage of first serves in, especially in doubles. Similarly, if the main pleasure you get in golf is to hit your drives farther than anyone else, then by all means focus your practice and training on hitting long drives. Do not expect to win very often though unless you spend time practicing the short game. If that rare home run is what keeps you coming back to play softball, then swing for those fences and ignore all those long fly-outs, pop-ups and strikeouts. If, for some reason, you want to win games, however, then you (and your team) need to focus on getting on base.

Maybe when the sportscasters say things like, "Well, Tom, I think the Twins could have won this game if they had only outscored their opponents," they really do have an important message for the sports fans out there. After all, I have never heard a sportscaster say, "Well, Tom, the Twins could have won this game even if they ended up with fewer runs if only somewhere along the line, one of them had hit a home run." Nope. Never heard that one. But I have seen people play as though that were true. Sadly, that does not just apply to weekend warriors. I actually saw a professional Yankee batter come up to the plate with the bases loaded and two out and proceed to strike out on three straight pitches. But wait. There's more. You have to understand *how* the bases got loaded. The opposing pitcher walked *three straight batters*. He had just thrown ten straight balls, none of them even *close* to the strike zone. But that didn't matter to our would-be hero. *He* was bound and determined to hit a grand slam home run no matter *where* those pitches were thrown. He swung and missed on three more terrible pitches. I am hoping that you can show a little more discipline than that Yankee did.

Focusing on what counts was touched on in previous chapters. It impacts developing your edge, how you allocate your training and practice time, as well as your strategy and tactics during the game. This is where an understanding of the game can be invaluable. Watching professionals can help here, but you must remember that the balance points among the various aspects of a game can be different at different levels and in different age groups. In professional baseball, the fielders almost always make routine defensive plays and sometimes make spectacular plays. The hitters can routinely hit a pitcher who "lost their stuff" or lost their control. Almost any runner can score from second base on a single. In amateur leagues, none of these "givens" is necessarily a real given. So what really counts can be different in different leagues and even against different teams. This often makes amateur athletics even more interesting than professional sports. If you are a center fielder, in an amateur league, you may be able to throw out a runner trying to score from second on a single. If you are a runner on second, and an outfielder is running for a sinking line drive, you have to be ready to take off if that ball is missed.

In watching professional tennis, you will certainly see some variations in the players in terms of whether they hit a one or two handed backhand, how fast their serve is, and how much topspin they put on the ball. But in amateur tennis you will see much more variation in skill levels and even how the strokes are produced. You will see tremendous variations in doubles tactics among various teams. So, in some ways, the amateur tennis player needs to be ready to adapt on more dimensions than the professional. By the same token, this means that developing and practicing your edge is even more important. If you have a very unusual serve for example, an amateur may not be able to adequately adapt during the course of a match. A professional, on the other hand, is likely to face that serve many times and will probably know about it ahead of time and may even have a partner serve in a similar way so they can practice returns.

Suppose that you are playing tennis against someone who hits a very slow high ball but consistently keeps it in the court. You might have trouble and lose the match and then say, "Well, if they would have hit the ball harder with more pace, I could have beat them!" You can say that. But it is very seldom the case in my experience that this then causes the opponent to say, "Ooops. Okay, you are right. You *should* have won. I concede." It might happen. But don't hold your breath.

CHAPTER TWENTY-TWO: TUNING IN TO TURNING OFF.

What do I mean by this alliterative phrase? I mean this. In most moves in most sports, there are a series of muscle contractions that provide the required power and speed. At any particular time, there are *many more* of those 720 muscles that are *not* needed for power and speed in that particular move. In fact, many of those muscles can *slow you down.* In the same way that you need to focus training and practice and strategy and tactics on what actually works to win games (or meet your goals), you also need to focus your moves on what *needs* to move and leave everything else out of it.

Moving other parts of your body or contracting other muscles will tend to add "noise" and "confusion" to whatever you are doing and slow you down as well as increase the chances of injury. For most people, it is more "obvious" to notice what they intend to move and to notice the muscles that are causing movement and much harder to notice little unintended moves and unintended tightness. So, that is what I mean by "tuning in" to "turning off." You need to learn to notice (during practice) not only the moves you intend to make but also the ones you do not intend to make. You need to learn to feel, not only the muscles that *cause* the movement, but those that are slowing it down. You need to relax and focus. At the same time.

Perhaps this is most apparent in golf because the person hitting a golf shot starts out still and the ball is not moving. You may be able to see, even without a slow motion replay, that the person is dipping or bending in an unnecessary way during their stroke. It is harder to catch this in moving sports. What is almost impossible to see, even in slow motion, is any tightness and contraction in muscles that are slowing the person down. At most, what you get is an overall impression that the professional golfer swings "easy" and yet the ball goes a hundred yards farther.

One way to help focus your movements on what is necessary is simply to practice a lot. Over time, your brain will have a tendency to cull out the unneeded movements. In some of your practice, it can be helpful to try to produce a very easy, loose relaxed feeling. During play, of course, having a relaxed but attentive mental attitude helps. You do not typically want to focus on the mechanics of technique during play but rather on your routine, your process and your goal.

More systematically, yoga, meditation, and deep relaxation techniques all help you "tune in" to a more aware yet more relaxed state of being. This can translate to a more aware relaxed feeling during play which will have the effect that you will have less tension in the muscles that would only slow you down by being tense. For some people, practicing to a musical rhythm helps. Having a consistent routine for pitching, serving a tennis ball, putting, shooting a foul shot and so on can be helpful as well. A consistent routine, in addition to other benefits helps prevent unnecessary and counter-productive movements.

In art classes, the student is taught to see the "negative space." This is the space *not* occupied by the objects. It is the space between objects. Similarly, you may find this analogy helpful in tuning in to the spaces between moves and the muscles that are to be relaxed during a movement. You may have to experiment a bit and see what works best for you.

CHAPTER TWENTY-THREE: MAKING LEARNING EASIER.

Why is learning a sport the least bit tricky? It should be easy, right? You can typically watch people who are experts perform either in person or on television. In most cases, you can even watch what they do in slow motion. And yet, learning to duplicate the results of the professional is often extremely frustrating. Why?

One obvious source of difficulty is that the winning weekend warrior may not have been born with the body of a professional athlete. And, even if you were, you may not have had the right kind of training and enough of it when you were very young. Now, as a weekend warrior, your "day job" or family responsibilities prevent you from spending the 60 hours a week practice that is necessary to make the professionals performance look "easy."

Another problem is that even in slow motion, you only see the movements of the professional. You do not see the brain signals and the timing of those signals sent out to the various muscles involved in a skilled movement. Of course, even if you *could* see such movements, they would not work for you because your brain and body are wired differently. Even two professional athletes are "wired differently." Despite many science fiction episodes in movies and television, the idea that you could simply "download" the program of someone else's skill and have it instantly be runnable in your body is … well, science fiction.

Of course, you can definitely pick up *something* about the required skills by watching professionals, particularly in slow motion. But you have to practice in order to translate that visual impression into the sequence of actions needed to make the smooth, graceful, correct motion needed.

In many sports, of course, it is not just *action* which is required but also *perception.* For example, you can watch a professional tennis player return a 125 mile per hour serve and maybe do a credible job of recreating the necessary motions to return a serve. But unless you can just as quickly and accurately predict where the ball is going as it leaves the opponent's racquet, speeds over the net, hits the ground and bounces up and away, you are not going to make a nice return. Similarly, you might be able to reproduce a nice smooth putting stroke in golf and that will clearly help. But you also need to learn to read the green and the grain in order to know where to aim and how hard to hit the ball. But if you are watching the pro hit a putt, how on earth can you tell what they imagined the ball would do and how hard they intended to hit it? Unless you are holding exactly the same club in exactly the same way, you would get a different result.

One thing that makes sports potentially less frustrating than some other kinds of learning is that you often get immediate feedback about your efforts. You swing a bat at a ball and you get a base hit, or you miss, or you hit a long fly out. You will know the outcome in a few seconds. Similarly, you hit a putt and it either drops, comes close or goes quite wide of the mark. You find out quickly. You hit a tennis serve and it lands in the service box, or it doesn't. You find out in a few seconds.

All that is well and good! Unfortunately, if you miss a putt to the left, for example, you do *not* typically know *why* you missed the putt to the left. Of course, your playing partner will be quick to say, "Oh, you pulled it." But that may not be correct. They are simply making conversation. You could miss the putt to the left for a wide variety of reasons.You may have misread the amount of slope. You may have misread the grain if it is Bermuda grass. You may have hit the ball off the center of the putter blade. Your putter may not have been going straight back and through. You might have been unlucky enough to have a puff of wind knock your ball off course. Or, your ball might have hit a small imperfection in the green. Or, you might have ever so slightly twisted the putter blade as you stroked the ball. You might not have been aiming where you think you were aiming Unfortunately, you do not normally know which of these is the issue. So, yes, in most sports you get feedback about *results* very quickly but unfortunately you do not get unambiguous feedback about the *cause* of an error. An excellent coach with a trained eye can certainly help.

In addition, watching your performance on video, especially in slow motion, can also help you determine "what you are doing." In golf, Dave Pelz developed a series of tools to help you determine what is going on with your putting stroke. For example, in one exercise, the instructor tapes a mirror to your putter face. Then, you take dead aim at a laser (which is turned off) at the other end of the room about twenty feet away. Now, the laser is turned on and you can see where you were really aiming. The result? No-one in the class is very close at all to being aimed correctly. Another putting aid is in the form of two prongs which you attach to the end of your putter blade. These prongs are just far enough apart so that if you hit a golf ball with the precise center of your putter blade, the path of the ball will be unaffected. But if you hit it ever so slightly off center, the ball will immediately carom off at a funny angle. Surprisingly, it is difficult to consistently hit the ball with the middle of the putting blade. With practice though, it can be done.

It would be nice to see similar inventions for other sports so that various errors could be interpreted more unambiguously. Slow motion video, as mentioned, does help some. If you are trying to improve your baseball hitting, for instance, you can see whether your misses are typically under or over the ball. Chances are that you will know that anyway based on whether you ground out or pop up more often. Unfortunately, the video alone will not tell you why you are hitting under the ball. Is the pitcher mixing up the spin and you are "guessing" a sinker when they throw a rising fast fall instead? Are you making some unneeded motion at the last minute? Perhaps you are dipping your shoulder and this brings the path of the bat too low.

A tennis serve, similarly, may go into the net for many different reasons. You may be tossing the ball too far in front of you so that almost any reasonable stroke will send it into the net. You may be whipping your wrist too early. But why is *that* happening? It might be that you are not really tossing the ball high enough to give yourself time to execute a good full swing. Again, practice and experimentation are vital and a good coach can definitely help.

One thing you can do with experimentation is to be a bit more scientific with it. Do not "experiment " by throwing the ball higher *once* and then judging whether this is good or bad based on a serve or two. If you think you may need to toss the ball higher, you need to do it till you are still tossing it consistently and you need to do it till you adjust your timing. *Then,* you should try a basket of balls and count how many are in the box. Only then will you have any basis for deciding whether or not to make this change.

There is another aspect of learning that we all need to understand. As mentioned, one of the things that makes sports fun is that you often get immediate feedback about results, even if the *reason* for the result may not be obvious. Having results quickly is important for learning. One thing that happens as a natural consequence of practice and experience is that you receive this feedback earlier and earlier. That is, if you are a novice golfer, you cannot tell whether you have hit a good shot until you see the ball land. A professional, however, can generally tell whether or not they have hit a good shot *immediately.* This means that they get faster feedback and can therefore learn more easily than a novice. The same is true in many other sports. An experienced basketball player "knows" as they make the shot whether they have executed it correctly. An experienced tennis player knows whether they have made a perfect toss for the serve early, and can even make a slight adjustment in the swing if necessary. In effect, the expert gets feedback more quickly than the novice and this, in turn, can make learning and adjustment easier.

There is, however, a downside risk of this. A few years ago, I was watching the Masters (a major golf tournament). At one point, play was interrupted because of significant rain (and more importantly lightning). The greens at Augusta where the Masters is played are notoriously fast. When play resumed after the rain, the greens were slower, of course. The pros, almost invariably left their putts short on the next hole they played. Okay. This is understandable. These generally fast greens were playing much slower than they had done when they had played their previous hole. But what happened on the second hole? The pros were still leaving their putts way short. Okay. It takes time to adjust. But what happened on the *next* green they played? They were *still* leaving their putts way short. How is this possible? These were professionals. They knew that rain would slow down the greens. How much they slowed down might be hard to judge so you might expect some putts to be short, some to be perfect and some to be long until they had adjusted to the changed conditions. But that is not what happened. For the entire rest of the round, the vast majority of putts were short. Why?

I believe that what happened with the pros is this: they had *experience* with putting the (typical) greens of Augusta from the earlier rounds, from practice, and in many cases from years past. As a result, they did not wait until the putt actually died to be get knowledge of their results. *As soon as they hit the putt,* they felt that they had hit it perfectly, at least with respect to speed, based on their previous experience. The putt "felt" right. Unfortunately, that positive feeling was a reinforcement for the putt they just hit and it happened much earlier than seeing the actual result. Therefore, their too-short putt was further cemented in their mind as being executed at the "correct" putting speed. Ironically, someone much less experienced with Augusta might have adapted more quickly.

Most of the time, the earlier reinforcement that comes from practice is your friend. But on rare occasions, when the conditions are quite different from what you expect, that early reinforcement can become an enemy. If you are experienced but used to playing only indoor tennis, for example, and now you are playing outdoors with a strong wind behind you, you might hit a number of shots that "feel" just right only to have them sail long. But before you see it sail long, you have already (in effect) said to yourself, "Nice shot!" You might be so surprised, you are sure your opponent is calling your good shots long. Be on the lookout for this when you are playing under unusual conditions and try to suspend your judgement until you see the final outcome.

CHAPTER TWENTY-FOUR: USING THE OFF-SEASON TO "LEAP-FROG" YOUR OPPONENTS.

Some people are lucky enough to live in the San Diego area where the weather is perfect 95% of the time year round. This means you can play golf, tennis, or softball pretty much all year (skiing and ice hockey, not so much). Many people, however, will typically only be able to practice a sport during part of the year. So, in the "off season," you may think that there is nothing for it. It is too cold to play golf so, sit back, watch re-runs of Gilligan's Island and wait for the spring thaw which is probably early April if you are the New York City area and early August if you are in northern Minnesota.

You can do that. However, you can also use the "off" season to improve your game even when you cannot play it. By doing so, while your potential opponents *are* watching re-runs of Gilligan's Island, you can leap-frog them. Some of the ways you can continue to improve are pretty obvious. If the golf courses are closed where you live, you can take a two-week vacation to a warmer spot and play! If that busts your bank, you can probably find a place to play "virtual golf" during the off season. You can almost certainly find a driving range that is open. If you cannot play outdoor tennis, you can probably find a place to play indoors several times a week. If you cannot play softball, you can still go to a batting cage a couple times a week. Even in Minnesota, there may be a day or two between that first October blizzard and that August thaw when you can play catch with a friend to keep your arm limber.

Beyond actually practicing the sport though, there are many additional things to do in the off season. You can certainly work on your mental game. Practice taking a positive mental attitude toward any challenge or set-back in work and personal life. Practice being mindful. Notice what is around you. Use your eyes and your ears. Notice how things feel in your hands and how your body feels as you walk, stand, and sit. Meditate. Practice cutting people a break. Instead of just getting angry when someone cuts you off in traffic, exercise your imagination instead and generate a number of reasons why they might be in a hurry. If you enter the next season with a positive mental attitude, your chances of winning are greatly improved.

Read about the game. Learn more about the history, the players, the rules. You will not only win more; you will enjoy the sport more deeply. You can watch slow motion video of the skills. Often, you can watch the professionals play. You can reflect about last season and set goals and make plans for next season. You can look at reviews of various potential coaches and teachers.

The off-season is also a wonderful time to increase your overall level of fitness. This not only gives you a jump on winning; it decreases your chances of injury. You can improve your strength, endurance, balance, and flexibility with additional focus on exercises specifically geared toward your particular sport. In fact, if you have limited time to devote to your sport, the off season may actually give you more opportunity for improving your overall conditioning that will the "on-season."

Another option, of course, is to focus on different sports for different seasons. You may prefer to play basketball during the winter and baseball during the summer and "forget about" the off season sport. If that aligns better with what winning means in your mind, that is fine too. Keep in mind though that even going to the driving range or the batting cage once a week during the off season will tend to keep you much fitter, lessen your chance of injury early in the season, and give you a head start on the season.

PART TWO: TACTICAL CONSIDERATIONS:

In the preceding section, we have dealt with strategy. Now, we turn our attention to the near term. How do you prepare for and play a particular match, game, or tournament? What can you do in terms of actions and attitudes to improve your chances of winning?

CHAPTER TWENTY-FIVE: PREPARE FOR A MATCH.

Naturally, the details of preparing for a match depend to some extent on the sport, but a surprising amount of preparation is very common across sports. We examine a number of these topics in turn. Regardless of sport, you want to know ahead of time about any particular conditions. In some sports, like golf, the conditions will vary a lot from one venue to another. Different courses are likely to have different weather conditions as well as different layouts, types of grass, and so on. Basketball courts will be fairly similar indoors although even here there can be important variations in backboards and floors as well as whether there are likely to be spectators. If you are going to play tennis, it is worthwhile to know the court surface in planning your game. Will it be outdoors? Will sun be a factor? What will the likely weather be? Do you have any choice in the matter? For example, if you are a younger player playing against an older opponent, you may be relatively better off playing in bright sun or under artificial lighting. If you are an older player, you may want to try to schedule matches when sun will be less of an issue. For physical reasons, an older player may find matches on concrete very hard on the body compared with those on clay courts.

You need to understand any specific rules for a tournament as well. For instance, in golf, there may be local rules that come into play. Something that looks like a waste area might be considered a bunker and something that looks like a bunker may be designated a waste bunker where you can move small rocks. Some courses may allow free drops from ornamental plants. Some tennis tournaments and leagues will play "no-add" scoring and have variations in tie-breakers. You are better off knowing these things before play starts. In softball, there are important variations among leagues. Some fast pitch leagues allow windmill pitches and some only allow a "figure eight" delivery. Some leagues allow stealing and/or leadoffs and some do not. Some play ten fielders; some, nine. There may be variations about pinch hitting and pinch running as well.

Assuming you want to play in the same venue more than once, you also need to understand the unwritten rules as well. Some playground basketball is very rough to the point where a "foul" is basically when someone sends another person to the ER while other venues are much more friendly. Similar variations exist in touch football, soccer, etc. If you are playing a contact sport with other people in your family or co-workers, you need to be especially mindful of the difference between what is allowed by the "rules" and what makes good sense. It may be a legal hit to smack your boss onto their back as forcefully as possible as they jump in the air to catch a downfield pass, but it might not good policy on your part. (See reference section for books on resume writing).

In many sports such as hockey, soccer, football, basketball, tennis, and baseball, it is extremely important to understand and prepare as much as possible for specific opponents. Professional teams have the luxury of having videos, scout reports, and even computer simulations to help them out. You will probably not have that kind of facility, but knowing what you can is still helpful. If you are playing a match that is particularly important to you, you might want to consider targeted practice.

Aside from knowing about your opponent and the conditions and rules, it is even more important to prepare yourself for an upcoming match. This includes mental as well as physical preparation. The amount and type of physical preparation depends on the sport, but generally you want to time your training so that you are in "peak" condition for your match, game, or tournament. This often means taking some time off from the most rigorous practice right before the event. You do not want to run marathons every day of the week leading up to a marathon! On the other hand, you might want to play golf every day up to and including the day before a tournament or take one or two days off. You will have to see what kind of schedule works best for you for your particular sport and taking into consideration your general physical conditioning and age. A day of rest might be good for baseball, softball, basketball, track, swimming, and tennis. You probably do not need it for optimal table tennis or croquet play though. If you are a softball pitcher, you may well be able to pitch day after day. An overhand hardball pitcher though typically needs at least three and sometimes four days of rest. Again, you will have to see what works best for you.

Weight training is good for almost any sport, provided you do it properly and in combination with flexibility exercises to make sure you stay loose. However, it takes two days to recover from a good weight workout so you probably do not want to lift weights the day of or the day before an important match. Stretching, flexibility, and balance are probably fine the day before and during. In just about any sport you want to make sure that you warm up enough before the game. Not warming up enough is far more likely to cause injury than over-exercising. I have seen many people go out and play some vigorous sport like tennis, softball or touch football and injure themselves almost immediately.

This brings us to another point. Make sure you arrive at the venue with plenty of time to assess the conditions and to warm up *thoroughly*. If google maps says it takes an hour to get somewhere, do not leave an hour before the match! The last thing you need before a match is to be stuck in a traffic jam worried about whether you will have to forfeit.

A very important last point of preparation before a match is to "align" or "polarize" yourself for the match and the sport. Basically, you want to avoid distractions and thoughts about other things and concentrate on what you are about to do. Some people find meditation a good way to do this. Others may get into it by having a set physical warm-up routine. Experiment and see what works for you. For most people arriving "just in time" before a game or a match and rushing out on the field to play is a bad idea, not only because you will not do your best, but because you are much more likely to be injured. Whatever your physical, mental, and/or spiritual routine is before a match, stick to it as closely as possible every time.

CHAPTER TWENTY-SIX: SIZE UP YOUR OPPONENT.

It is the nature of sports that there are one or more opponents. If you want to win, it only makes sense to spend some time and energy understanding your opponent(s). How much your success depends on understanding your opponent(s), however, depends a lot on the particular sport. In most golf formats, you are playing an entire field and more depends on how well you play than on knowing the particularities of your opponents. In softball or football, the entire team is facing another whole team. *If* you can find out about the opposing team, so much the better, but often you will not have the resources. Obviously, pro teams will scout opposing teams extensively. In the case of football and basketball, they will not only understand the strengths, weaknesses and current condition of the major players; they will also understand the offensive and defensive plays. Baseball does not depend so much on set plays, but there will be scouting reports on pitchers, hitters, and so on. It is doubtful that as a winning weekend warrior you will be able to gather a huge amount of intelligence about opposing teams ahead of time.

In track, biking and swimming — among other sports —- although who will win varies somewhat from day to day, if A is consistently faster than B and B is consistently faster than C, then A will be faster than C. But this does not necessarily happen in tennis, basketball, boxing, football, soccer, hockey, baseball and other sports where the moment to moment play depends on the *interaction* between the teams or players. In these sports, it is quite possible for A to consistently beat B and B to consistently beat C and yet C may beat A. It is in these kinds of interactive sports that you *most* need to understand your opponent. Of course, even in sports like track, biking and swimming, it is important to know about your opponent, but the number of factors you need to consider is smaller. In particular, you need to know whether an opponent is capable of "out-kicking" you at the end of a race and by how much so as to make sure you are too far ahead to be overtaken. On the other hand, if you are a better sprinter, you need to be in enough contact with the runners ahead to be able to make up the gap at the end of the race.

Regardless of the sport, you probably will not know a huge amount about your opponent ahead of time (as a winning weekend warrior). But you can certainly begin to size up your opponent once you see them arrive on the field of play. Even during warm up you can begin to see their physical conditioning and characteristics. You can continue to watch and learn during the entire game or contest. Keep mental track of what is working against this particular team on this particular day. I have never understood why many amateur softball and baseball teams sit on the bench and pay *no attention* to the opposing pitcher. Most amateur pitchers are very consistent in their behavior and may well have particular mannerisms that "give away" what they are about to pitch. Many amateur league hitters are also somewhat predictable. Typically, only a few if any opposing hitters have the power to hit over the outfield for instance. And many of them are consistently pull or push hitters. You will find a huge discrepancy in fielding abilities as well. On a particular amateur team, the third baseman may be able to pick up any grounder and zing it accurately to first base while the second baseman bobbles half the grounders that come to them.

The specific observations you want to make depend on the sport, but here are some example observations from tennis doubles. Some people are very quick to poach while others very seldom poach at the net. Once you figure this out, you can use this information to decide whether to hit a return of serve cross court, down the line or lob over the net person. Sometimes an opposing team will have one person who is a slow runner. You can obviously make life difficult by lobbing from one side of the court to the other, at least until both players play "back" at which point, a drop shot to the less mobile player can cause trouble. Some players, to avoid having a lob go over their head, will never step in closer than the service line. This makes it difficult to lob over their head, but it also means that you can shoot right to their feet. Generally, this forces a weak return. Some players (actually an astounding number) try to hit the first serve with all their might and just poke the second serve over. Be prepared for that poke. If the serve is short as well as soft, you can hit a drop shot, smack the ball into the net player, lob over the net player's head, or hit a sharply angled shot. It is critical though that while you *commit* to a shot, your eyes remain on the tennis ball as you strike it.

Amazingly enough, I have sometimes asked tennis players about the opponent that they just played and they cannot even tell me whether their opponent was tall or short, fast or slow. Most of the time you want to play to the opponent's backhand, but you will sometimes run into players whose backhand is stronger and more reliable than their forehand, so you need to keep track of that and adjust accordingly. Some players favor their forehand so much that they try to "run around" every shot to the backhand side and hit it with their forehand. This provides you an opportunity to hit wider and wider angles to their backhand and when they are far enough off the court, hit a winner to their forehand. Some players will avoid the net at all costs. In such cases, obviously you want to draw them in and then pass or lob over them. Other players however relish the net and hit well-angled volleys for winners. So, if at all possible, you want to force them back on or behind the baseline. None of this is particularly subtle rocket science. But it does require some observation.

Some players, when they have a chance to put the ball away at the net will almost invariably hit it down the middle while others will tend to hit a drop volley. Others will try for a sharp angle. If you notice such consistent patterns, you can use it to your advantage by anticipating the shot ahead of time. Of course, other players will vary their response. In that case, it is even more important to keep it away from the net player!

Now, let's assume that you have not personally bought a million copies of this book to keep it out of the hands of potential opponents. In that case, you can safely bet that somewhere along the line, you are going to be facing an opponent who *also* read this book and so, while you are trying to assess them, they will be trying to assess you! What can you do? I provide some advice about misdirection in chapter twenty eight, but first, let us take a look at the need for adaptation.

CHAPTER TWENTY-SEVEN: THE NEED FOR ADAPTATION.

If something consistently doesn't work, you need to change it. Chances are, I am not even the first person to mention this to you. But apparently, it is still worth writing this advice, because I have seen people in many sports do something that is *clearly* not working and then just keep on doing it. To be fair, I have also seen this in every other endeavor in life as well. So, it is not a phenomenon limited to sports. Let's look at adaptation.

Adaptations take place at different speeds. For example, if you have always batted righty, you are not going to be able to "adapt" to an opposing pitcher by successfully batting lefty for the first time in your life. Similarly, if you are playing tennis and your opponent is "teeing off" on your serve, you will not find much success in suddenly trying to hit the ball twice as hard as you have practiced. These two *are* examples of something you might try to change over the course of months or years.

However, there are many things that you can adapt *during* a game or contest. In my experience, people do not. You can gain a winning edge simply by being someone who *does* adapt. Not adapting seems to be a uniquely human characteristic. As the story goes, if a rat learns that the cheese is in the left side of a maze but then the cheese is shifted to the right side, the rat will be confused for a few trials but will quickly discover the cheese on the right and then look for it on the right side. A

134

person may continue to go left insisting that this is where the cheese is *supposed to be.* Other people may focus their time and energy trying to determine whose *fault* it is that the cheese is no longer where it "belongs" or cursing the rotten luck they always have with cheese.

I mentioned before that, in general, people should be trying to hit singles in softball or draw walks. Instead, many people step up to the plate determined to hammer a heroic homer. Okay. They can be forgiven the first time, because they may be in that tiny minority of folks who made the grave error of not buying and reading this book. But even if they had *not* read my book, you might think that after they had gone up to the plate twice and tried to hit a homer and hit a long fly out the first time and a pop-up the second time, they would now *try something different.* For instance, they might just spontaneously and all on their own try to get a single. But no. In my experience, not so much. Instead, they will try *even harder* to hit a home run on their third and fourth at bats.

Equally astounding to not changing something that is failing is the number of times sports teams *do* change something that *is* working. The "prevent defense" in football is perhaps the most notorious and most frustrating to fans. The home team plays "regular" defense through the first 47 minutes of the game and is ahead 28 to 14. Now, however, to "insure" a win, they go into a "prevent" defense. This would be better labeled an "allow" defense because it allows the opposing team to gain first

135

down after first down. The team that only scored two touchdowns in the first 47 minutes of the game now scores two more touchdowns and a field goal in the last 13 minutes of the game!

If pro teams *sometimes* do this, amateur teams do it in *spades*! In nearly every sport I've seen where the outcome depends on the interaction pattern between the teams, I have seen a team who is winning by using one interaction pattern change it to a different interaction pattern and lose. Maybe the players are just getting bored? Maybe the winning team wants to make it more "exciting" by letting the score even out? Maybe the players are just plain tired of hitting winners and instead bloop the ball back into play? Maybe, maybe, maybe? I don't know, but if you figure it out, please let me know so I can say more about it in the next edition.

CHAPTER TWENTY-EIGHT: USING PRIMACY TO YOUR ADVANTAGE.

I know this will come as a real shocker to you, but guess what: human beings are not perfect information processors and decision makers. We are subject to all kinds of biases and distortions and prejudices. Maybe you cannot *change* human nature (and anyway, that's what I'm trying to do) but you can make *use* of human nature to your advantage. As it turns out, the various kinds of distortions and biases that people make are very similar regardless of age, gender, upbringing and so on. If you understand even a little of what these biases are, you can use that to influence your opponent to make bad decisions. Of course, you might decide that this particular way of winning is not for you. And that is fine too. It might be considered by some to be just too much in the way of gamesmanship and "head games." Then, you might want to skip to the next chapter. Or, since some of your opponents may employ these tactics, you may want to read the rest of this chapter anyway to make sure you are not having the wool pulled over your eyes.

The "primacy effect" is a good place to start. It is a psychologist's way of saying that first impressions are important. Let's say that the first time you meet someone they are polite, clean, well-dressed and full of energy. You get an impression of this person as someone who has their act together. The next time you meet them, however, they are unshaven, slovenly, and silent. What you will *not* tend to do is

revise your opinion of the person *in general.*
Instead, you will tend to try to find a reason why
this polite, clean, well-dressed person is having an
off day. Perhaps they are hung over? Or, sick?
Maybe they are depressed about something at
home or work? Conversely, suppose the first time
you meet someone, they are unshaven, slovenly
and hardly say a word. You form an impression of
this person as being rather out of it. Suppose the
next time you meet them they are instead clean,
well dressed and polite. You do not instantly
change your opinion. Again, now you generate a
story in your head about why this slovenly person
now looks different. Perhaps they are going for a
job interview? The point is that the first impression
tends to be a lasting impression. Eventually, of
course, you may change your opinion, but not
quickly.

So, how does this apply to sports? Let us take an
example from tennis doubles. Suppose you are
starting a set and you hit your first two serves at
moderate speed with nothing special on them.
Your opponents now think: "Well, this person
serves easy. I can make a great return." If you now
start adding heat and spin, they will tend to think:
"Oh, an ace. That must be an accident. I already
know this person's a weak server." Similarly, if you
hit the first few serves to the forehand, this is what
the receiver will come to expect. You can
"surprise" them by hitting serves to the backhand.
After hitting the first few serves to the forehand,
you can keep up the "illusion" that you are hitting

to their forehand even if, from then on, you only hit 1/3 or 1/4 of the serves to the forehand.

You can turn prejudice to your advantage. People will tend to judge you by how you look (just as you judge them). If you are short, they will tend to think it will be easy to lob over your head. *If* you are athletic enough and can develop a good jump and smash technique, you will putting a lot of balls away. It will be difficult at first for people to overcome their prejudice regarding short people. Similarly, if you are *fast* but old or overweight, it will take time for people to discover that you can run things down. If you are a woman with a better game than your male partner in mixed doubles, you will find that most opponents require many games to discover that they should have been hitting the ball to the guy all this time. By then, the match may be over.

Another phenomenon that you can sometimes make use of is contrast. For example, if someone throws a 100 mile an hour fast ball, you can be sure that their 60 mile an hour change up pitch is a lot harder to hit than it is when it comes from someone who throws a 75 mile an hour fast ball. If your tennis doubles partner tends to hit a flat drive while you put a lot of spin on it, that makes it more difficult for your opponents to adjust to your spin.

CHAPTER TWENTY-NINE: PREDICTION AND MISDIRECTION.

There is another way that primacy comes into play and that is to use the beginning parts of an action sequence to mislead your opponent. In some sports; for example, golf, running, discus, shot put, javelin, weight lifting, bowling, and swimming, there is very little benefit in trying to "fool" your opponent into thinking you are doing something different from what you are doing. Instead, you want to keep your routine as constant as possible. And, there are some *parts* of other sports for which this is true as well; e.g., kicking a field goal in football, or shooting a foul shot in basketball. What is important in those cases is to focus on your routine and try to execute it consistently. However, in other cases, you want to *begin* a routine the same way but then, as late as possible, change what you are doing so that your opponent is misled about your actions. For instance, in football, you want to disguise your offensive plays as much as possible and as long as possible. A baseball or softball pitcher wants to disguise their delivery so that the batter cannot tell ahead of time which pitch is about to be thrown. In tennis, if you are going to hit a good drop shot, you want to disguise that fact by starting the backswing the same as if you were hitting a hard drive. If you are trying to score a goal in soccer, you do not want to "telegraph" to the goalie where you are kicking. The same goes for a hockey shot or an overhead smash in tennis. In table tennis, you want to have a variety of service spins that "look the same" from across the table. In basketball, you want to be able to fake one way and break the other direction.

There is another thing to say about being unpredictable. If you are *too* random, you may just encourage your opponent not to over anticipate but instead to take a Zen stance of taking whatever comes and reacting to it. (That's the stance *you* should take.) Instead, you want to repeat patterns enough to set up an expectation in your opponent's mind and then break the pattern. How many repetitions it takes to set up an expectation in your opponent's mind is difficult to predict ahead of time. However, you may get clues to this from their behavior. If you hit three tennis shots cross-court and you see your opponent start to "hang out" there before you hit your fourth shot, then, you have your answer. If you hit two table tennis serves with top spin and the first shoots over the end of the table but the second one hits near the back edge, then it is time to hit what looks like the same serve with backspin. Generally speaking, across a wide variety of sports, I find most people begin to build up an expectation after 2-4 repetitions. Of course, their expectation will be even stronger after more repetitions of a pattern, but you will not benefit because, in the mean time, they will have begun to anticipate too well what you are going to do and that will give *them* an advantage.

CHAPTER THIRTY: COMBINING FORCES (DON'T BE A JERK).

A general tenet of military strategy is to have superior effective "force" at each engagement. Of course, "force" is not just the number of troops but also what kind of training, ability, and weaponry they have at their disposal. The word "effective" is important as well. If your opponent commands 10,000 troops and you only have 2000 similar troops but your 2000 possess highly superior mobility then they can race around and beat smaller segments of your opponents forces 1000 at a time. At each engagement, you would actually be outnumbering your opponent two to one.

In sports, "force" can be a useful concept in at least two ways. First, physical force plays an important part of many sports. If your football linemen have superior physical force, they can push back the other line. If you can hit a tennis serve with more force than your opponent, then, other things being equal, you will have a large advantage. If you are vying for rebounds in basketball, if you can apply more force, you can position yourself more effectively than your opponent. If you can apply more effective physical force, you can jump higher and longer, throw the shot put farther, and lift more weight. If you can apply more force to your hockey slap shot, you will hit it faster and it will be harder for the goalie to save. If you can apply more force in a golf drive with the sweet spot of your driver, you will hit farther and typically have an easier second shot.

142

In all of these examples, however, superior force must be applied *effectively*. If you charge the opposing lineman blindly, they may be quick enough to deflect you with their hands and you will just be lying on the ground. It does no good at all to hit a 125 mph serve in tennis if you double fault 55% of the time. It does no good to apply more physical force in basketball if you foul out in the first period of every game. Even a faster slap shot will not do you much good if it is always completely predictable. To be consistently effective, superior force must be applied *intelligently*.

In addition to actual physical force, the concept of psychological force also plays a crucial role in most sports. But first, let's look at how superior physical force is generated. Mainly it is done by applying the right muscles at the right time. Most athletic moves require the use of many muscles. The effective force requires that each muscle come into play at the right time. In a golf swing, for example, many beginners are most conscious of their hands (probably because we use our hands so much in daily life). They may begin the swing with their hands and eventually, the large muscles of their trunk and legs come into play. This results in lots of energy expended but little effective force and not much club head speed. Instead, a fast and effective swing needs to begin with the legs and end with the hands. Similarly, power in the tennis serve largely derives from the legs and torso. Of course, snapping the wrist at the end is vital as well. I have seen tennis players copy a very complicated service motion and then come to a complete stop before finally hitting a wrist and forearm only serve! Since all momentum from the legs, trunk and arms is gone, there is no point at all in the earlier motions. They may as well stand stock still and just hit an arm and wrist serve in the first place.

Adding (or, sometimes multiplying) forces together can generate enormous power if done correctly. Although a lot of force is generated by the correct timing of contracting various muscles at the right time, there are at least two other potential sources of force. For one thing, muscles are "springy" so that a muscle stretched will tend to store force as they are stretched. As an example, when a golfer turns their shoulders (and sometimes hips) away from the ball, that backswing stores energy in stretched muscles. In the downswing, the energy that is stored in the muscles is released along with the additional force generated by active contraction. It is also important that muscles antagonistic to the addition of forces be as completely relaxed as possible. Otherwise, "tension" in these other muscles will tend to slow down the baseball swing, the golf swing, the soccer kick, the tennis serve and so on. In many cases, forces are first stored and then released in the equipment as well. Perhaps the most visually obvious example is the extreme bend in a modern pole vault. Another common example is that in a forceful golf swing, the head of the golf club "lags behind" the shaft. If timed correctly, the bent golf

144

club will straighten out just as the golfer is adding all their own forces to the velocity of the club head. This "spring" action of the golf shaft adds still more velocity to the club head. In golf, the ball is sitting still as it is when a basketball player initiates a foul shot or when a bowler begins their motion or when a soccer player makes a free kick. However, in other sports, something may already be in motion before you add your own force to it. In baseball hitting, the pitcher throws the ball with considerable velocity toward the batter. As the batter hits the ball, that force is added to the recoil off the bat. In other words, even if the bat is held rigidly and still in front of a fast pitch, the ball will carom off the bat with some velocity. This is still more true in tennis.

There are many applications of adding forces in various sports. If you watch a major league baseball pitcher, it becomes immediately clear that they are not getting all their velocity from their arms alone. They are using their legs, their torsos, their shoulders, their triceps and their wrist snap with proper timing. And, as in the golf swing, they are adding recoil force to positive force. As they throw their leg up and push off the rubber, they are leading with the body while letting the hand and arm "lag behind." This causes stretching like a rubber band and when they snap forward they are adding the force of the recoil to the positive force they are generating with their muscles. Similarly, if you watch a slow motion video of a professional tennis player hitting, say, a forehand, their racquet and wrist initially go *backward* relative to their arm.

This causes a recoil which is added to the positive force. Of course, as in the baseball pitch, the legs and torso swing are added to the arms to generate more force.

Another obvious example of the positive addition of forces is the play of a baseball outfielder when they need to catch a fly ball and throw home to try to catch a tagging runner. They do not sprint to a fixed position under the ball and then catch and throw home. The outfielder positions themselves so that they are running forward as they catch the ball so that they can add their running speed to their throwing speed. Similarly, a volleyball server runs forward to the back line before hitting a jump serve.

Sometimes, the addition of forces can be troublesome if you are not careful. For example, in tennis, if you need to run forward quickly to hit a volley, it is easy to hit it beyond the baseline. You must take into account that your running velocity is added to your volley speed. A little more subtly, if you are running hard for a backhand say from the middle of the baseline directly to the backhand corner, there is a component of your running speed that is actually *away* from your intended target. You have to hit such a shot especially hard to get it deep over the net and aim farther to the right than you normally would. For this reason, *if there is time*, it is better to take a slightly curved path to the place where you hit the ball so you can be running toward the net or at least be stable when you hit the ball.

146

In some sports, the addition of forces includes elements of nature. A long fly ball with the wind behind it can be a home run while the same ball into the wind is a long fly out. In tennis, a high "perfect" lob can easily go long if there is a tailwind. This is especially tricky if the wind is above the windscreen and you may not even feel it at ground level. You should check out flags or trees above the windscreen for a read on the wind. In golf, because the ball can be in the air a long time, the wind can have a very large effect. In Hawaii, for example, it is not unusual to have a two or even three club wind meaning that if you hit the ball with the wind you need to use two or three clubs less while if you hit into the wind you need to hit two or three clubs more. It can be especially tricky when the winds are swirling or are going different directions at different levels. More than once, I have "relied" on the two club tail wind which has been blowing constantly only to have it die out completely during the time my ball is in flight! Plop! On one occasion, I was hitting a mid-iron uphill while a very stiff breeze was in my face. I hit a "perfect" shot only to watch it sail far over the green. This was sad because the area behind the green had long uneven grass and the green itself was pitched severely back toward the fairway. Even a perfect flop shot could easily roll off the front of the green. As I walked up the hill, the wind shifted and indeed, at the top of the hill, there was a strong wind 180 degrees from what I had felt at the bottom of the hill. Now I know to look at treetops near the green to see what is

147

happening. Wind can be different anywhere but this is particularly likely when there are nearby changes of elevation.

Wind can affect a ball in any outdoor sport, but it may be particularly problematic in golf. Hitting into the wind makes a person want to swing all the harder to "make up" for the wind. This *seems* logical, but the probable result is that you will put more spin on the ball and make a poorer swing. If you hit into the wind even a slight tendency to fade or draw will be exaggerated. If you are skillful enough to choose, a low draw will fare a lot better into the wind than a high fade which basically will generally go nowhere good when hit into the wind. Many instructors recommend actually swinging a little more slowly (with more club) while hitting into the wind.

While physics explains the addition of mechanical forces, mental and psychological forces also can have a tendency to "add up." If you are tired, and nervous, and having some bad luck, these forces can also "add up" to conspire against your playing your best. All you can do is to focus on what you *can* change which is what you are telling yourself and thinking about while you play. At each point, instead of dwelling on past mistakes or calling yourself names, it is even more important under these circumstances to play one shot at a time and focus on going through your routine.

So, at this point, you may be wondering why this chapter is also called, "Don't be a jerk." This advice is not about your personality, although for maximum enjoyment in sports, you probably do not want to be too much of a jerk too much of the time. What I am referring to are the dynamics of movement. Obviously, sports are heavily involved in movement. You move your body; often you move an implement like a club or bat or racquet and often you cause a ball to move as well. Another way to think about movement is that it is a change in location over time. The faster you change your location in a given amount of time, the faster your velocity. In most sports, having the ability to move yourself or your bat or the ball faster is a huge advantage.

In many sports, it is not only important to think about moving quickly, it is important to think about the *rate* of *change* in velocity, also called acceleration. Imagine you are riding on a train or bus and standing up without holding on. As long as the ride is smooth, it is easy to keep your balance, no matter whether you are riding a bus going thirty miles an hour or a train going seventy miles an hour or an airplane going six hundred miles an hour. On the other hand, acceleration —- or change of speed —- you definitely feel as a force. As the plane takes off, it accelerates and you are pressed back in your seat. If you are standing on a bus and it accelerates, you need to "brace yourself" against that force. You can do this, up to a limit. At some point, too much force and your body (or even your car) will be smashed.

Acceleration is important in many sports. For example, a running back not only requires a relatively fast running speed, but they need to accelerate quickly up to a fast running speed in order to get through a hole quickly. In hitting a tennis ball, if you accelerate your racquet head as you hit, you will have more control. Hitting the ball off center from the sweet spot will have less effect on your shot if you are accelerating the racquet as you hit.

"Jerk" is a change in acceleration. If you are standing on the bus and it is accelerating smoothly, you can brace yourself against the force of acceleration. But if the bus driver suddenly changes from accelerating to slamming on the brakes, it is the *change* in acceleration that will throw you on the floor. In sports like golf where it is just you and the ball, you typically want to accelerate smoothly. In other words, you do not want to "jerk." When people say that someone's swing is smooth, this is what is meant. They accelerate throughout the swing. As in tennis, if you hit a golf ball slightly off center but your club is accelerating as you make contact, the effect of hitting slightly off center will be small. On the other hand, if you are slowing down or decelerating as you hit a drive or a putt, any small error will be greatly magnified. This is why you do not want to use "jerk" — hence the phrase, "do not be a jerk."

However, the story gets a little more complicated when you have an opponent who is reacting to your movement. If you are playing basketball and all your moves are "smooth" with no sudden changes, it is true that you will be in better control; however, your moves are also easier for your opponent to anticipate. They can more easily block your shot or steal the ball. In basketball, it makes sense to *suddenly* change direction. In golf, however, the golf ball is *not* trying to get away from you. It is *not* trying to anticipate your swing and dodge out of the way (though many golf swings look as though this is just what the golfer is thinking).

Tennis provides an example of a sport that includes both aspects. For maximum control, you want to hit the ball with smooth acceleration and have no jerk at all. However, for maximum *surprise,* you want to be able to change the direction of your swing (and therefore the ball) at the last moment because this gives your opponent the least time to react to your shot. To make matters even more complicated, the tradeoff between these two factors (control and surprise) depends on the situation. If you and your opponent are both at the center of your baselines, you mainly want to hit smoothly and powerfully. You are not going to gain much by "suddenly" changing the direction of your shot, and you are going to greatly increase the chances of your mis-hitting it. On the other hand, if you are at the net about to hit an easy volley and your opponent is running full tilt to their forehand to cover your volley, change quickly to aim the volley behind them, and you will likely hit a winner.

In baseball, the hitter should concentrate on making smooth acceleration. It is silly to try to "jerk" the bat in order to change from pushing to pulling the ball. The fielders are so far away and so spread apart that you are not going to increase your chances of hitting in a gap between fielders, but you will increase your chances of striking out. On the other hand, if you are bunting, you may be able to effectively change direction at the last second.

In football, as in basketball or soccer or hockey or volleyball, it is a great advantage to be able to change direction at the last possible split second after your opponent has committed. The topic of when to employ "jerk" and when not to is complex and varies from sport to sport. It also varies according to your level of fitness. "Jerk" tends to put a relatively great amount of stress on your joints and tendons compared with smooth acceleration. We will explore these topics in more detail in future books dedicated to specific sports. For now, just think about and watch how speed and changes in speed and even changes in acceleration figure in your sports. Then see how you might use these insights in your own games.

CHAPTER THIRTY-ONE: NEVER GIVE UP.

Why would you? What is the point? You can *influence* the future with a positive or negative attitude, but you cannot *completely control it,* and you cannot *predict it.* Never give up. Never assume that the other player or the other team enjoys all the luck, better abilities, better strategy and there is no way you can win. You *never know.* Momentum can shift. A key player on the other team may have an unexpected physical problem. You may find a new tactic that works. For example, in tennis, you may be playing a player who hits every hard shot of yours back twice as hard. They hit twice as many winners as you. They make half as many unforced errors. They are winning every single game! Then, instead of trying to "outgun" your opponent, you hit high looping shots deep to their backhand. They try but fail to return these just as they were doing your hard drives. Suddenly you are winning a lot of games.

You are playing baseball and no-one on your team seems able to hit the odd submarine delivery of the opposing pitcher. You are down 5-0 in the fifth inning. But hopefully people have been *watching* this pitcher even when they are not batting or on deck. When they come up for the next at bats, people have figured it out. Now, they are hitting him or her regularly. Or, inning six rolls around and he or she completely loses his or her control. Nobody *needs* to get hits. the pitcher walks in two runs before being relieved with a more conventional (and hittable) pitcher.

You are playing basketball and the opposing team sinks three three pointers in a row and is leading 9-2. What does that mean? Not much! Unless you and your teammates convince yourselves that it means you can't win. If you stay positive and focused, your chances of winning are excellent. If they can sink three three-pointers in a row, so can you. They can miss six shots in a row. People can foul out. Okay. But what if there is one minute left to play and the score is 95-6. Now, surely you should count yourself out.

Why? There is no point to counting yourself out. It will be more fun and better practice if you play the last one minute believing you can still win. And, it is actually not impossible to win the game. The team could be disqualified, for example, because it turns out that an ineligible player was playing for them or failed a drug test. Of course, that is a hollow victory, but the point is that, no matter what, you cannot predict the future. Furthermore, you will play better if you never count yourself out.

Here is a true story from my own tennis adventures. I played in an industrial league and ran across someone who was playing pretty much flawlessly. I was playing well that night but my opponent won the first set 6-0 and he was up 3-0 in the second set. I could not find any way to lob, pass, drop shot, ace or otherwise do more than come up to deuce. Then, midway in the second set, I returned another one of his awesome serves short, blocking it back to the service line. He ran in and hit a hard topspin forehand … into the net. He missed an easy shot. Well, *that's* no big deal. Every pro on tour has done that! But this guy threw his racquet on the ground and began berating himself for ten minutes! If there had been an outside referee, he probably would have been warned or disqualified. But we were our own line judges and so on. Finally, we got back to playing. You know what? I won. 0-6, 6-3, 6-2. Of course, as you probably recognize, *I* did not beat *him*. *He* beat himself. But that is another possible outcome in any sport. Never count yourself out! Never give up!

In the 1980 Winter Olympics, the USA team of college kids was a huge underdog slated for a certain loss to the much more experienced Russian team. But guess who won? USA! In 2004, the Boston Red Sox were down 0-3 in the World Series against the New York Yankees. This was an "impossible" deficit to overcome, even without the "Curse of the Bambino." But the Red Sox *did* win anyway. In 1950, the USA soccer team were 500-1 shots underdogs against England. But the USA prevailed, 1-0. In 1993 (American) football season, in the AFC Wild Card game, the Buffalo Bills were down 35-3 to the Houston Oilers in the second half. Frank Reich, the back-up quarterback had to come in for the injured Hall of Famer Jim Kelly. The Bills' star running back Thurman Thomas had to leave with a hip injury. Surely, if there was ever a good time to give up, this was it. But they did *not* give up. Reich won with *four* touchdown passes.

If these kinds of upsets and comebacks can happen at the top level of sports, I assure you that they are even *more* likely for you as a weekend warrior. The variability is greater among players on an amateur team. The variability of performance from week to week is greater because weekend warriors typically cannot put the same consistency of hours into the sport that a professional or even college athlete can. The role of luck is *greater* for you. Never count yourself out.

Of course, this philosophy does not just apply to sports. Ever hear of Ray Kroc? He started the MacDonald's franchise. His biography is fascinating. He failed at several careers before becoming a billionaire. Think of Nelson Mandela. He was the president of South Africa. But first, he was imprisoned for 27 years! Just guessing, but I would say it would be far more tempting and "reasonable" for him to give up after, say, twenty years in prison during Apartheid than it would be for you to give up when you are behind in your golf match or your softball game. Everyone knows the story of Thomas Edison and the many attempts to improve the light bulb. This same kind of thing is *generally* true when it comes to advances in technology. It isn't easy or obvious at all! Sure, there are some insights and breakthroughs along the way, but to make better computer chips, displays, toasters, auto engines, movie cameras — it takes lots of work! And, *none* of these improvement and inventions that we take for granted today were the result of someone giving up! Of course, you may have to give up, at least temporarily, on a particular *way* of achieving your goal. You might have to give up on following your serve to the net when playing against a particular opponent. But you never have to give up on winning. Even more importantly, you never have to give up on yourself.

CHAPTER THIRTY-TWO: PLAYING WITHIN YOURSELF.

While it is a good idea never to give in, never to give up and never to count yourself out, it is also a good idea to "play within yourself," at least most of the time. While we have all heard this phrase, what does it really mean? It means that you have to try to choose and execute plays and shots that are in the realm of what you can actually do. It may sound obvious, but I have seen many people playing many different sports attempt low percentage stunts that are unlikely to impossible.

One example I have already mentioned several times. Amateur slow pitch softball players insist on trying to hit home runs even when there is no fence. They mainly hit long fly outs but sometimes hit pop-ups or actually strike out. They very seldom hit home runs. It isn't necessary to hit home runs in slow pitch softball because nearly everyone on your team can learn to get a base hit most of the time. But these kinds of heroics are not limited to softball. In tennis, as I mentioned, I see many players who attempt to hit an "ace" on their first serve while missing 95% of them. Then, they "poke" their second serve weakly into the service box. The problem with this strategy is that such an easy second serve can easily be hit for a winner or at the very least put you at a very strong positional disadvantage. This is especially true in doubles. If you consistently poke your second serve in, the receiver can typically just hit hard right at your partner at the net making for a very difficult shot for them to handle. It would be much better to hit the first serve with some spin and/or speed that enables you to get at least 60-70 per cent in and then follow up with a second serve that still shows some action.

Another common mistake in tennis is to try to hit a winner "one shot too early." You have your opponent on the run. They hit a weak return to the service line. You run in from the baseline and instead of pressing your advantage by hitting a hard angled shot that will put your opponent even farther out of position, you take your racket back as far as you possibly can and swing just as hard as you possibly can aiming for the precise corner of the court. You will most likely hit this shot long, but you might hit it wide. Often you hit it wide *and* long. Of course, sometimes you hit such a shot *way* long and hit the back fence. Not surprising, since you are "swinging for the fences." On ten percent of the cases though, you fool everyone and instead hit it into the net. And then, there is that five percent of the time you really do pull off that clean winner. Ah! Now, *that* feels good. And if you goal in playing tennis is mainly to have that good feeling once every couple weeks, go for it! On the other hand, if your goals are to win more often than losing or to improve your game, then instead, "play within yourself" and keep pressing your advantage. You don't want to lose the advantage and just play a completely easy safe shot back to the middle. But you do not have to hit a ball that is out of reach of Rafa or Roger. Because you are not playing Rafa or Roger. You are playing Joe who is 62 years old and will be unable to reach the next shot or the one after that if you keep pressing your advantage. Do not suddenly switch sports from tennis to jousting where you feel it necessary to "kill" your opponent or the ball.

Similarly, I have seen many net players "go for" a volley in the middle of the court that is diving over the net and that they have to hit way below the level of the net. Their doubles partner has plenty of time and space to take the shot but the net player decides to grab it instead. Bad things happen even if their partner doesn't kill them right then and there. Of course, if a return comes back slow and high and you can take the volley well above the net, that is an entirely different matter and there you *should* hit an aggressive shot. You *still* do not need to hit a shot with all your might however; you just need to hit a winner or something close enough to a winner that it will force another very weak shot.

In golf, I have seen many attempts at miracle shots. Half of the ones I've seen were by Phil Mickelson early in his career before he decided to win tournaments rather than perform miracles. But the other half were attempted by ordinary golfers and their results were no more often miraculous than Phil's. There are many types of miracle shots. Of course, the most common is the "If my grandson can hit a 300 yard drive from the back tees then so can I" tee shot. The way it works is this. You tee off behind someone who hits a beautiful 300 yard tee shot that splits the fairway. You generally hit your tee shot about 220 yards, but you calculate that if you just swing about 50% harder you can outdrive this other golfer! Ugly things typically result. Not always the *same* ugly things, but ugly things. You top the ball. You sky the ball. You hit a pull hook. You slice the ball out of bounds. And so on. If your grandson hits the ball 300 yards and you hit it 220 yards, the solution is to tee off from a different set of tees, not to swing with all your might. Or, if you are in a tournament that requires you to tee off from the back tees, then you need to make up for your lack of driver distance with accurate shots to the green and an excellent short game. You will never consistently achieve that extra 80 yards just by swinging harder.

Of course, there are times when miracle plays are your only choice. If your basketball team is behind by two points and you are at mid court right before the final buzzer, yes, you try for the mid court three pointer. That makes more sense than dribbling the ball up another twenty feet and hearing the buzzer signify that you just lost by two points. If your football team is down by five and you only have one play from your own five yard line, you had better hit that bomb. If you are in a figure skating or gymnastics competition, you might go out on the ice or the matts for floor realizing you need to land a very difficult maneuver in order to win. But these occasions are rare (except in movies). And rarer still are times when such miracle play is called for but not attempted. Far more common are the occasions when there is no actual need for a miracle play but people attempt them anyway.

One of the major root causes as to why people try for miracle plays is that they are basing their actions on what they *should* be able to do as opposed to what they actually *can do.* A person may say to themselves, "I should be able to jump up three feet in the air and *nail* this overhead!" And, maybe they "should" be able to. When they were twenty. And practiced four hours a day. Playing within yourself means instead of playing with how you think you should be able to play, that you make an honest, reality-based assessment of your actual current skills and play based on that assessment.

Of course, making that assessment means that at some points you "test yourself" in order to see just how high you can jump for an overhead, how hard you can hit accurately, and so on. The time to do this is during practice or in a match that you are sure to win anyway. That's one reason why practice should never be "lackadaisical" or "casual." You should always being trying hard to reach that drop shot or run back for that lob. Otherwise, how will you have any idea what your own limits really are? Similarly, in batting practice, by all means, spend a few of your swings trying to hit a home run. Keep track of how well that goes. Spend most of your batting practice trying to hit very precise targets between the outfielders. This will give you some idea how accurate your placement is.

If you want to try to hit a 300 yard drive on the driving range, by all means, go for it. But keep an honest track of how many times you succeed and how accurate those drives are. Put your hand at arm's length and spread your index and middle finger. Now see how far apart those points appear to be on the driving range. That is the range within which your drives should land on a typical hole. Hit ten drives going for the fences. If one of them makes it 300 yards and stays within this imaginary fairway, great. Now you can make a reasonable estimate of how likely it is for you to hit a 300 yard drive in a match. One out of twenty. That's right. If you can do it one out of ten times on the driving range, cut that in half for your chances during actual play. Why? Because on the driving range, as I already pointed out, you are hitting ball after ball with the same club and you have no real pressure. You will hit a drive and then 30-40 seconds later you hit another drive. In real play, you will hit a drive and then wait 15 to 30 *minutes* before hitting another one.

CHAPTER THIRTY-THREE: YOUR TEAM SUCKS — NOW WHAT?

If you have the option, you may want to consider getting on another team. But sometimes, you are on a team because the nature of the league or tournament put you on a team and you have no choice. Or, sometimes, you are on a softball or basketball team mainly because you want to play with your friends or workmates. It just so happens that your skill level is a lot higher than that of your teammates. Now what?

First of all, if you do have a higher skill level, you might help others improve. For beginners, even a little practice can help a great deal. Often, people with little experience may join a golf team or a basketball team or a softball team for social reasons and believe that they are "awful" when they simply haven't had much practice with the sport. The good news is that their skills can quickly improve with knowledge, training, and coaching. In our softball team at NYNEX, we had several players who were new to the game (and the country). Most of them were cricket players. Cricket players can almost always pick up softball batting quite easily because hitting a cricket ball is actually more difficult. On the other hand, they had no idea whatsoever about how to run the bases. This is where having first and third bases coaches comes in handy. First, the first base coach needed to remind them not to carry the bat to first base. Then, the coaches had to tell them when and how far to try to run as well as reminding them to "stay connected" to second or third base if they were stopping there. For people who grow up watching baseball, base running is fairly "instinctive" but for people learning the game, it turns out that it is actually quite complicated. What to do depends on how many outs there are, whether you are ahead or behind in the game, and how the ball is hit. In addition, in amateur leagues, the quality of the fielding is so variable that what to do also depends on the catching and throwing skills of the person fielding the ball. You might well be able to tag up and run home from a very short fly ball caught twenty feet behind first in right field when it would be sure suicide in the majors.

Of course, it is important to distinguish coaching during practice from coaching during play. During practice, you might well give suggestions about how to hit, field, or throw — especially if someone is relatively new to the game. However, these kinds of suggestions made in the heat of play are disastrous. There is no time to think consciously about a different way to do something during actual play. In some sports, such as baseball, football, basketball, or tennis there are natural breaks during which there is plenty of time to discuss strategy and tactics, but never motor skills! No matter how well-intentioned, do not attempt to change your teammates swing, motion, etc. during a competition. (Or yours either for that matter, if your main goal is to win).

Even when it comes to strategy and tactics, a problem also arises when your teammates already think they know the answers and do not really want to take coaching advice. I've played tennis doubles with older players who play "net" at the service line. They are afraid to stand closer partly out of a fear that the opponents will lob over their heads and that they won't be able to run back in time to return the lob. In such cases, I say something like, "I can cover lobs all over the court, so if you feel comfortable, feel free to move closer to the net." I give them the option, because even though it may make more "theoretical" sense to play closer to the net, if my partner lacks confidence there, then they will probably do better in their preferred position.

Similarly, in a scramble or best ball golf competition, it is best to try to discuss but never dictate another's shot. Even if your partner is trying a "miracle shot" over a considerable expanse of water, if they are convinced that is the shot for them, don't undermine their confidence by saying there is a lot of water or that a layup is a safer shot. (I can pretty much guarantee that if a lay up is your idea, they will hit that layup long and into the water). But it is not untoward, *before your partner picks a club,* to say, "what are are options here?" If they say they can hit a two iron a couple hundred yards over the water onto the green, say something to improve not reduce their confidence. If they are going to make that shot at all, it will require a very relaxed swing. Any muscle tightness will just diminish the chances of success.

In most sports, it is useful to have a captain who makes the strategic and tactical calls. It doesn't due to argue about these every time. If the quarterback wants to go for a bomb on third and short, they do not need a parliamentary debate about it. In football, there is a designated quarterback who calls the plays. In tennis and golf, it is useful to pick someone ahead of time to call the plays. This may not be absolutely required but the last thing you want to do is start arguing in front of your opponents. Sometimes, it is important to communicate *during* plays. This is always important in volleyball, football, tennis doubles and so on, but particularly so when your team is just learning. Sometimes, newcomers need to be encouraged and reminded that it is okay to shout during sports events! It does no good to whisper "got it" or "mine" if the others on the team cannot hear it. Of course, by pre-arranged agreement, these shouts can also be used to mislead the opponents.

In dealing with being on a team of low skilled folks, it helps once again to think about your goals. If it is more important to you to play with your friends, you may decide to stay on this team and help out as best you can to improve everyone's play. But you may also take the opportunity to chose what aspects of your own game are most important to focus on. If your tennis partner is very slow, for instance, you may decide that a good thing to focus on is to improve your court coverage. You may want to run for balls you normally wouldn't. The advantage for you is that you may improve your endurance and your skill at hitting the ball while running at full tilt. The advantage for your team is that you may win more points. However, you do not want to push this to such an extreme that you are actually trying "miracle shots" when your partner has a perfectly good shot. For example, let's say you are playing tennis and at the service line on the deuce side. A fairly hard shot is hit to your opponent at the baseline. It streaks over the net and sinks quickly to land at the service line on the add side. But you decide to try to intercept this by jumping to your backhand and trying to hit a volley from well below the net because you are, after all, a much better player. Bad idea! Even if you do manage to get to this ball and keep it in play, you are going to hit a very weak shot. Of course, you may poach more when your opponents are trying to hit everything to your weaker partner. But that doesn't mean you should try to hit every possible shot.

Similarly, it is really bad form, no matter what your skills, to try to cover left, center, and right field from center field by running full tilt to take a ball away from another player when it is obviously "their ball" even if the chances of your making the play are greater than theirs. Such grandstanding completely undermines team spirit no matter what the outcome. And it certainly reduces the skill and confidence of the player whose ball you steal. You may make a great running catch and get that particular out, but you have damaged the overall chances of your team's winning on an ongoing basis. A ball hit in the gap between an excellent fielder and a mediocre one is another matter. Sure, have the better player call it and have the weaker player back them up. By the way, this advice is not just applicable to baseball, football, and tennis but to all of life's "games."

CHAPTER THIRTY-FOUR: DEALING WITH YOUR WEAKNESSES.

It's one thing to deal as objectively as possible with your team's weaknesses. It is even more difficult to deal with your own. But deal you must. Your weaknesses can be dealt with on both a long term and a short term basis. In the long run, you can deal with weaknesses by practice, weight training, aerobic training, stretching, coaching, and, if necessary, even changing sports, venues, or partners. In the short run, you most deal with your weaknesses through the use of intelligent strategy and tactics while keeping a good mental attitude.

In order to make either or long term or short term adjustment to your weaknesses, of course, the first order of business is to understand what those are. When I say "understand" your weaknesses, I mean to make an *accurate* assessment. Judging from how infrequently people actually do this, it must be hard. What most people do is one of two things. First, they may completely *deny* that they have a particular weakness. About halfway through a round of golf, they have hit one fairway. On hole ten, they again slice their drive off into deep rough. Then, they say something like, "I don't understand it! I actually hit good drives almost every time at the driving range." So, there you have it. This person, *in their mind,* possesses no weakness when it comes to hitting the driver because, when they are hitting driver shot after driver shot on the driving range, they do well. As already explained, it is much easier to hit the driver when you are doing it every 45 seconds than when you are doing once every 15-30 minutes.

The second common strategy that people opt for is to *exaggerate* their weaknesses. "Oh, I cannot hit a good drive to save my life!" Perhaps you have heard, "I *cannot* sink a putt today." This "woe is me" over-generalization strategy is not limited to golf of course. In basketball, you might hear, "I cannot hit my jumper today." In tennis, it might be, "I cannot return a serve today!" In baseball, you might hear, "I cannot hit a thing today! I must still be in a slump." If anything, the over-exaggeration strategy may be worse than the complete denial strategy. But neither approach counts as taking a realistic view of your strengths and weaknesses.

There are several root causes for these extreme positions. First, let's face it: life is complicated. Modern life is especially complicated. There is a tendency to over-simplify, to sort fifty shades of gray into two categories: Black and White. You see it in politics and economics. Why would we not expect to see it in sports?

Second, it takes you "off the hook" in one of two ways. If you *deny* a problem, it takes you off the hook because you don't have to go through the work of trying especially hard to fix it or work around it. If you *exaggerate* your problem, you are *also* taking yourself off the hook. If you *cannot* hit a drive or sink a putt or hit your jumper nor return a serve, then you don't have to try hard. You also avoid disappointment.

Whatever the reason, whether in sports or any other aspect of life, it is useful to make a nuanced and realistic assessment of your skills. But you have to be careful not to "jump to conclusions."

The most extreme example of exaggeration occurs when people jump to the conclusion that they are not good at a sport and give it up —- after a few attempts! I have asked people, just to be sociable, whether they play golf and their answer is: "Oh, no, I tried that a couple times." A couple times?! If that were their strategy as a toddler, they would never have learned to walk. As infants and small children, we spent countless hours learning to walk and talk and then to read and write. Yet, somehow, as adults some of us believe we should learn math, programming, and sports in a short period of time. If we have any difficulties, we conclude we have no ability to do it!

Let's assume you are wise enough not to fall into that error. But you might still suffer a more mild case. For example, you may find it more natural to pull a baseball or softball into left field if you are right handed. You might find that the first few times you try to hit to the opposite field, you have more difficulty. That is natural, but it doesn't mean you *cannot* learn to hit to the opposite field. Or, you might be golfer who is deadly afraid of the sand because you (think you) cannot hit it out of the sand. Every sport for every player will have some

172

things that seem to come naturally and other things that require more practice. However, do not conclude on the basis of a few attempts or lessons that whatever you are trying is a permanent weakness.

On the other hand, if you have spent a fair amount of time working on your tennis backhand and it is still not as consistent and strong a shot as your forehand, you might accept that, at least for now, your backhand is a relative weakness and you need to work around it to some extent. On some shots, if your footwork is fast, you can "run around" your backhand and hit a forehand. You might find that a sliced backhand works well for you. You can "cheat" a little bit when you position your body so that you are somewhat toward the add court sideline (for a righty). Of course, at the same time you are trying to deal with your weakness, you opponent, if they are wise enough, will be trying to exploit your weakness. Once they "catch on" that you have little confidence in your backhand, they will try to hit every shot to your backhand or move you farther and farther toward the add court sideline and then try to hit a winner out of reach wide to your forehand.

If you are a golfer who consistently tries to improve your driving length and accuracy but are still missing 60-70% of the fairways, you might consider several ways to deal with this weakness until you are able to improve your accuracy. You can play from more foreword tees. You might consider that you will score better if you hit a five wood or a four iron off the tee. If you play well, you might be scoring an extra stroke on most holes, but that 90 is still a lot better than a score where you are hitting three or even five off the tee. If your tee shots are not missing the fairway by much, you might also make some effort to hit a good second shot out of the rough. Often players who miss the fairway with their tee shot will compound the error by trying to "make up" for hitting in the rough by trying to hit out with a three wood or three iron. More than likely, this just results in a really bad second shot.

While it is reasonable and realistic to work around your weaknesses, it is not very effective to dwell on them *during play.* It is just *boring* if every time you miss a tee shot, you say, "I just can't hit the driver" This just makes your playing partners think, "no kidding" or "then why don't you hit a five wood off the tee or play from more foreword tees" or "okay, but don't whine about it." If you whine enough, your playing partners may construe this as asking for advice. This is a penalty in golf and pretty much a bad idea in any sport. Another and related ineffective strategy is to think consciously about every tip you've ever heard while trying to execute your problematic shot.

It works like this. You slice your first tee shot into the driving range on the right. So, you think to yourself, "I must have had an open club face." Quite possibly, but now is not the time. So, on the second tee, you decide to change your grip to make it more closed and you hook your ball into the water on the left. So, you think, "maybe I should open my stance a bit to compensate." Now, on the third hole, you slice the ball again. And, you think....See there's the trouble. There is a time and place for thinking! But too much is a bad thing; especially when you are not basing any of this on *facts.* You probably cannot tell, after the fact, what the root cause of your slice was and how to fix it. A good pro might be able to in a playing lesson. On the other hand, you can be consciously aware of what club you are hitting. If you are playing in dense moist air and you are consistently hitting the ball ten to fifteen yards short of your intended target, you may want to re-think your club choice in order to compensate for the humid air. By the same token, if you are playing at 8000 feet, you might notice that you need to club down from what you usually do.

In other words, there are some kinds of mistakes or weaknesses that you might be aware of and be able to correct between points. For instance, if you are playing tennis and find yourself in "no-man's land" a lot and you are losing a lot of points mishitting the ball off your shoelaces, you can resolve to make more effort to be at baseline or net as much as possible. But once you start thinking about what the weakness is in your *form* on the serve, backhand, or forehand, you are probably guessing. Similarly, if you are in the middle of a hockey game and trying to change the form of your slap shot, you are probably skating on thin ice. Generally, you can become aware of and change weaknesses in strategy and tactics during the contest while there is a short break in the action. Generally, you will not have accurate information about what you are doing wrong in your motor movements and even if you did have accurate information, it will be very difficult to change that effectively on the fly during an athletic contest.

If you suspect that you have a flaw in the details of the way you are performing a motor movement, the best time to address that is between contests, hopefully with the aid of a good coach, or at least with the aid of a video camera and slow motion. You might become aware of and fix a problem in your stance or a deviation in your routine. For instance, if you generally set up square in your golf swing and on this particular day, you notice that you are putting your left foot ahead of your right *and* you are pushing your shots, yes, you do want to go *back to your normal routine.* But don't try to invent a new one. Not during play.

CHAPTER THIRTY-FIVE: COVERING ALL THE BASES — OR NOT.

Dealing with your weaknesses may easily slide into insisting on not having any; that is, being *perfect.* This is something to strive for, but do not expect to attain it in the first half of the twenty-first century. Even the pros, let alone weekend warriors are unlikely to make every putt, hit safely at every at bat, fan every batter, or nail every jump shot. And there is a perfectly good reason for this. The sport itself is *designed* to be challenging! It actually would be a lot less fun if it allowed perfection on a regular basis. There is no "natural reason" that a golf hole must be so narrow! It could be as wide as a basketball hoop. Then no one would miss short putts or even moderate putts. And golf would be a lot less fun. On the other hand, the hole could also be 1/8 inch wider than a golf ball. Then golf would be so frustrating no-one would play it. Similarly, there is no natural reason for the size of a basketball hoop. It could be as wide as soccer goal. But then no-one would miss shots from inside mid court and basketball would be no fun either. There is a *reason* it is impossible to reach perfection in sports. Sports are *designed* not to allow it. Yes, improve. Yes, strive for perfection. But remember that sports are designed to prevent perfection.

There is a more subtle version of expecting perfection and it is here named, "covering all the bases." In football, you cannot provide *ideal* defensive coverage against the long ball, the flank pass, the screen pass, the option play, the sweep, the reverse and the draw all at the same time. In tennis, you cannot be in a perfect position to return a serve to the body, to the forehand, the backhand, a slice, a kick serve, a hard flat serve, and a short serve all at once. You might be able to position yourself so you have a good chance of returning all these serves. And there are certainly places to stand that tempt your opponent to take advantage of your position. Similarly, try as you might, you cannot position your nine or ten baseball fielders so that no-one will ever get a base hit. You probably could do it with twenty good fielders but then baseball would be a long series of outs with an occasional home run.

Generally, sports are designed so that you are forced into making tradeoffs and decisions. You generally cannot be equally and perfectly prepared for all contingencies. You therefore have to focus on the most likely or the least damaging. You position your baseball outfielders at a depth and position so that most balls hit to the outfield will be fly outs but a few will fall in for base hits and a very few will go into a gap between fielders for extra bases. You position yourself in tennis near the baseline so you can return most hard hit drives. You may not be able to reach a perfectly executed drop shot but so long as you keep the ball deep, this is difficult for your opponent to pull off. If you hit a shot that only goes to the service line, you are subject to a drop shot, but also subject to a sharply angled winner and a deep shot that lets your opponent take the net. Once you hit the short return, you are in trouble and you cannot "cover all the bases."

In business, companies must also decide where to focus. Are they going to focus on particular service sectors, products, or geographical areas? Are they going to try to differentiate themselves through great high touch customer service? Or, are they going to try to invest in new technology and differentiate themselves through having the latest and greatest? Or, are they going to focus on cutting costs and become a low-cost provider? Any of these strategies can work. Unfortunately, some companies are overcome with a deadly combination of fear and greed. They decide they will do *everything*. In this case, they will do nothing well enough. They decide they will lower costs but not lower prices. Instead, they will try to convince their customers that they are low cost, high quality, with good customer service by spending money on a ferocious PR and advertising campaign. Such a ploy may work on a very short term basis, but people are too smart to fall for this in the long run.

Similarly, if you are a weekend warrior and try to do absolutely everything and cover all your opponent's options, you will end up doing nothing very well and not cover any of your opponent's options well enough. This is a losing strategy in sports, in business, and in life. Focus and commit.

Because it is impossible to "cover all the bases," another important strategy is to use the geometry of the sport to force your opponent to "cover more bases" than you do. In tennis, for example, if you keep your opponent pressed back behind the baseline, the number of options they can effectively execute is relatively small. If, on the other hand, you return a ball short to the service line, you have gifted your opponent many more options. As already pointed out, from the service line, they can easily hit a drop shot or a deep shot to your forehand or your backhand or hit a steeply angled shot to either side. In the football option play, the quarterback can throw a pass, lateral to another running back or run the ball themselves. This makes it hard for the defense to cover all the contingencies. In hockey, if you outnumber your opponents because of a power play, clearly it will be much harder for them to "cover all the bases." Similarly, in basketball, if you can execute the fast break effectively, your team will outnumber the opponents near their own basket and they cannot guard all your options effectively.

CHAPTER THIRTY-SIX: TIMING.

Timing is clearly critical in sports. It may be less obvious that timing works on many levels. In terms of motor skill, timing is critical in the sense that your speeds and forces can only be added or multiplied optimally if each action comes into play at the right time. That is why, when you observe a top notch athlete execute a high speed tennis serve, a 350 yard drive, a jump shot, a dunk, or a double back flip, it appears so effortless. If you hit your tennis serve sixty miles per hour, each of your muscles may be just as strong as or even stronger than someone who can serve 120 miles an hour. They are almost certainly not four times as strong as you are. But their *timing* makes their *effective* strength in that complex movement much greater.

Okay, you ask, but how do I improve timing? Having the right timing depends on a number of things. First, it is important to execute the movements in the right way in the first place. For most people in most sports, this requires getting good instruction in the proper technique. You *might* be able to pick this up by watching a really good athlete or by experimentation but for most, having a good teacher or coach is important. Second, you need to practice. Third, you need consistency. Once you determine a "right way" to execute a movement, you need to practice that way for quite awhile to gain consistency in timing. At some point, you may decide to modify your technique. But if you modify it every day or even every few minutes, you will never achieve proper timing.

Consistency is not just about the actual execution of movement though. You must go through a consistent routine before execution, and ensure that your body is in a consistent state. This helps make your timing more consistent and ultimately closer to the proper sequence. If you play on a full stomach one day, on an empty stomach the next, and hung over on a third day, you will find it very hard to achieve any consistency in timing or in results. By the same token, you should keep up a consistent workout plan with respect to your play, especially when you are learning. If you are stiff one day from lifting weights while you practice your serve but not the next time and then your legs are sore the next time, you will tend to get inconsistent timing. If you wear sun glasses one day and not the next, this will tend to change your timing as well. Similarly, if you keep varying your routine, at batting, on the mound, on the tee box, before a putt, before a serve, or before making a foul shot, you will tend to get very inconsistent results. With extended experience, you will learn how to adapt to changes in internal and external conditions. You will be able to compensate so as to keep consistent timing. A professional athlete who needs to play all the time will adapt faster than a weekend warrior.

Your routine should not only be *physically* identical time after time; your routine also needs to be *mentally* and *emotionally* identical. Obviously, your mental and emotional state varies somewhat depending on circumstances, but extreme emotional swings depend more on what you tell yourself about various events in your life rather than on the events themselves. Finally, learn to relax every muscle that is not actively involved in executing a movement or in providing the platform for the movement. Excessive tension in other muscles will tend to slow you down and provide additional sources of variability in your shot, swing, pitch, kick or stroke.

Some people find that using a metronome or listening to a specific piece of music or mentally saying a particular catch word or phrase on every occasion will help make timing more consistent. When it comes to a constant routine, it is important to remember eye movements as a part of this. For instance, if you are shooting a foul shot, it is important, not only to dribble the ball, say, three times before each shot, but also to have a constant sequence of looks; for example, basket, floor while dribbling and quick glance at the front of the rim before shooting. In general, it does not matter precisely what the sequence is so much as that it is consistent. Similarly, before you hit a putt, you may look at the hole every time while making two practice swings, look at the ball, take another quick look at the hole right before hitting and then back to the back edge of the ball. At the same time, it is useful to think the same thing every time as well such as: "In it goes" or "smooth and easy" or whatever. If you are constantly varying what you think about and where your eyes go from foul shot to foul shot or from putt to putt, you will introduce a lot of variation in your timing.

All of this being said, it is no doubt true that some people "naturally" are more consistent in their timing than others. Some people are able to move more quickly than others. These are probably two of the characteristics that enable some people to become professional athletes. As a winning weekend warrior, you may not be blessed with the kind of nervous system that makes speed and consistency of timing easy, but you can still improve. There is no point in obsessing over what you cannot change. You need to focus on the things you can do to improve your timing. Sometimes, watching a video or getting a particular image in mind may help. For instance, it might help you in a tennis serve to watch pros serve, both in real time and in slow motion. Or, it might help you to imagine you and the racquet are a whip being cracked or that a bolt of liquid lighting begins in your feet, rises through your body, out through your arms and hands into the racquet and electrifies the ball. Or, you may notice a particular feeling or sensation in your shoulder or hands when you hit a particularly effective serve. You want to try to recreate that feeling every time.

CHAPTER THIRTY-SEVEN: MANAGING YOUR ERRORS.

Newsflash: You will make errors. Even the professionals make errors! In fact, even the *very best award-winning professionals make errors!* That's right! People who are lucky enough to be born with extraordinary talent, get taught by the very best coaches, and work 60-80 hours a week for twenty years to hone their skills *still make errors.* As explained before, sports are *designed* to make errors inevitable. A sport in which people played "perfectly" would not be fun and would not, in fact, be a sport at all. If you would like to play such a sport though, you can make one up easily enough. How about "Drop the Penny in the Wastebasket." Here's how it works. You take a large waste basket at least a foot across. Now, you get a penny out of your pocket. You walk up to the waste basket and you drop the penny into the center of the wastebasket from a height of about one inch above the rim of the wastebasket. This is a lot like basketball! Only easier! You won't make any errors! I am also guessing that you will not find it to be much fun. I am guessing that however much you enjoy this "sport" for the first month or so, you will not be playing in ten years.

So, for *most* people, even though they are surprised or even shocked when they make an error; even though they may get frustrated or even angry when they make an error; in fact, a sport easy enough to avoid errors is *not fun.* Most adults get no satisfaction from repeatedly dropping a penny into a wastebasket even if (or especially because) they do it correctly 100% of the time. So, the first step in managing your errors is to recognize that they are not only inevitable but that they are a necessary part of the sport.

The second step in managing your errors is to realize that your emotional response to an error is not hard-wired into your brain the way a knee jerk reflex is. It depends on how you view the error. If you think of it as an inevitable part of the game and an opportunity for learning how to do better, you may be slightly frustrated, but you will not break into profanity over it. Ironically, an amateur may well have a more overblown emotional reaction to missing a six foot putt with nothing but ego riding on it than a professional golfer who just lost two hundred grand by missing the putt, or indeed, failed to make the cut at Q school for the entire next season. If you do make an error, the focus of your thoughts need to be on what went wrong and how to fix it for next time. In some cases, there may be nothing to fix. You might have just had bad luck. Perhaps you were putting on a day that was dead calm and one stiff stray breeze sent your putt astray. That can happen. But generally, you broke your pre-shot routine, or misread the green, or pulled your head up too soon to see the results. The most important aspects of managing your errors are not to get overly upset about them and to see what you can learn from them. In addition, although an error, however "important," is not cause for suicidal thoughts, you *do* want to make the next putt, shot, jump, throw, serve, kick, slap shot, or stroke with supreme confidence!

There is another sense in which it is important to manage your errors and this means adjusting your strategy and tactics to make your errors cost you as little as possible. If you are playing tennis singles for example, and you just drew your opponent completely out of the court on the deuce side causing them to hit a weak blooper back to the center of the court, you *could* decide that this is an excellent time to show off your skills and hit the hardest possible volley at the sharpest possible angle to hit the outside edge of the line. That will be a real winner…if executed flawlessly. And, if you are up 2 sets and 5 games to zero and 40 love, why not? However, in most circumstances, it is sufficient to hit a volley with moderate pace into the add corner, giving yourself a foot or so of margin in depth and angle. Then, if you do happen to make a slight error, the ball will still be in play and most likely still be a winner.

In golf, you may find yourself 250 yards from the green and ready for your second shot on a par four. The fast, backward slanting green is guarded by generous front sand bunkers on the left and right with only a narrow throat of ten yards between them. Your longest three wood ever hit is 260 yards. So, you *could* try to hit a three wood up onto the green. And you *could* call it a "bad stroke" if you end up in the sand with a very difficult up and down shot. A better analysis (assuming you are not one of the top fifty golfers in the world) is that your "error" was not in *executing* the stroke but in *choosing* the stroke. You are much better off to hit a club that cannot land you in the sand and that gives you a nice distance for a short pitch or chip onto the green.

Managing your errors does not mean always taking the safe way. Sometimes, you must make a risky play. Certainly, in the example above, if you are in *match play* and your opponent just hit their second shot to within a foot of the flag, you should go for the miracle shot. In tennis, you do not want to hit every shot so tentatively that you never make a mistake but you also never pressure your opponent. But playing smart and managing your errors does mean that you make a realistic assessment and play accordingly. Play with *confidence,* but play with some humility as well.

Lack of realistic humility is not limited to sports. It is amazing how many otherwise intelligent business people decide that they have no need to pre-test their product or service to find out how to improve it; that is, to discover what the mistakes are so they can fix them. Instead, they presume that they have designed their product or service perfectly (because they are such a genius) and there will be no need for testing. Sigh.

CHAPTER THIRTY-EIGHT: YOUR SOCKS
BELONG ON YOUR FEET; NOT UNDER YOUR
ARMPITS.

Of course, you may find various teaching aids
useful in improving your skills *before* a match in
any sport. In golf, for example, the Medicus really
can give you feedback about "jerking" the club
rather than smoothly accelerating it. I have already
detailed why you might find Dave Pelz's various
gadgets useful in learning to putt better. Golf
seems particularly fertile ground for growing all
sorts of businesses around teaching aids.
However, there are many aids for other sports as
well. The important thing to remember about
playing aids is to leave them at home when you
begin an actual match.

In many sports, training aids are illegal during play.
Even if they are not, they will prove a distraction
from using whatever level of skill you have.
Perhaps the most egregious case of such aids is
the guy who tried to wear an extra pair of socks
under his armpits during a round of golf.

My wife and I were invited to an outing sponsored
by American Express financial advisors at the
Garrison Golf Course in New York (with beautiful
views of the Hudson). We were paired in our
shotgun start with two folks with considerably
higher handicaps than ours. But beyond that, one
of these guys had been cautioned that it was
important to keep his arms near his body during
the golf swing. As a reminder, his instructor had

189

told him to put socks under each armpit and make sure they didn't fall out during his swing.

Somehow, the instructor forgot to mention that this was just a training aid and not something he should take out onto the golf course. So, here is this guy on the tee. He puts these socks under his armpits. Takes a practice swing. The socks fall down. He picks up the socks and again places them under his armpits. Takes a practice swing. The socks fall down. He picks up the socks and again places them under his armpits and takes a practice swing. The socks fall down. I think you get the picture. Finally, he manages to hit the ball off the tee and it rolls about twenty yards, generally about halfway to the forward tees. Sigh. And, it wasn't just for tee shots. The socks were there for mid-irons, chips, and sand shots as well as putts. As you can imagine, we were by far the last foursome to finish and came way late to the putting contest. Please. If you have a training aid, do not bring it to a match. You should believe in your swing, your stroke, your shot, yourself and play with whatever talent and luck you have that particular day.

Mental aids are a little more subtle than physical training aids. It might be worth having a *little bit* of mental aid during actual play. But too much mental aid is still a heavy burden to bring to a game. For most people, it might be worth bringing *one* mental aid to an actual sporting event. For example, if you have a tendency during your tennis to stop watching the ball, it might work for you to remind yourself to watch the ball while you are waiting for your opponent to serve. But it will be counter-productive to think about your grip, your racquet head preparation, watching the ball, keeping your knees bent, shifting your weight, turning your body, keeping a loose wrist, firming up at the moment of impact, making a nice follow-through, keeping the ball away from the net player, keeping the return deep, coming up on the ball to generate topspin, reminding yourself to stay hydrated, noticing which way the wind is blowing, and calculating the speed of the earth's rotation while waiting to return serve. If you *do* think about all that your opponent will be able to ace you with a 40 mph "cannonball."

If there is one thing worse than bringing your own training aids to the golf course, or the baseball diamond, or the horseshoe pit, or the tennis court, it is bringing them for someone else. You really need to keep well-intentioned advice for team-mates to a bare minimum at most. In almost every case, the best level of "training" for your team-mates *during* play is zero.

CHAPTER THIRTY-NINE: POST-MORTEM — WIN, LOSE, OR DRAW.

One of the most important parts of any competition comes after it is over. At some point when you are relaxed physically but still recall pretty well what happened, it is time to take stock and examine what went well, what could have been done better, and what needs to change for next time. Of course, if you are a professional athlete or playing on a Big Ten team, you will have video, statistics, and coaches to help with this debriefing. But even if you have none of that support, you can still go over the match mentally and learn from it. This does *not* mean beating yourself up for losing or gloating over a win. It is not about ego. It is about reality.

Some of the questions you ask yourself relate back to your plan of action. Did you prepare properly for the event physically, mentally, and strategically? What parts of that worked? How can you do better next time? For example, if part of your preparation was to improve your cardiovascular fitness, were you able to play the entire time without undue fatigue? If not, can you increase your endurance further? If you feel you are at the edge of what you can achieve given your physiology and time constraints, and you found yourself out of breath, what else can you do to compensate? Did you keep up a positive attitude during the match or did you find yourself delving into anger, depression, or anxiety about the outcome? If you kept on a pretty even keel, how did you manage that? If not, how can you improve your emotional state next time? These are all examples of questions. There are many variations depending on the sport and what your goals are, but the overall point is always the same. What went right? What went wrong? How can you do better?

Of course, answering these questions intelligently requires that you have done some thinking about your goals. If you easily trounced your opponent and your goal was *only to win,* then you may have had a great success. But if your goals included honing your skills or getting in better shape, you might consider finding a more competitive match next time, even if it increases your chances of losing.

While it is useful to set goals ahead of time, after a match is also a time to reflect on your goals and how you feel. For example, you might have as a goal *only winning.* Now you won a landslide victory, but you don't really get any joy out of it. Or, maybe you had an awesome contest and lost in the end but you feel a sense of elation. You may want to revisit your goals. Winning *per se* does not elate you; but having an all-out competition does. It is important to understand what gives you pleasure because that determines your next course of action.

Regardless of the "big picture" changes you might want to make such as seeking out harder (or easier) opponents, a competition also gives you a chance to reflect on what you can do better tactically. If you were playing volleyball, did you try for too many "miracle shots"? If you were playing ping pong, did you have too many unforced errors? Or, were you too conservative thus allowing your opponent to slam winners too often? What did you learn tactically? If you were playing baseball, were runners thrown out on the base paths? Did batters swing at bad pitches?

If you have extremely good recall, you might be able to replay a sporting event enough to consider improvements to your mechanics as well, but most people will not be able to do this reliably. You will often notice professional golfers and tennis players "replay" a stroke *immediately* after an error to try to understand what they did wrong. This is not bad, provided you can immediately refocus on playing the game. If you start obsessing about your grip or your stance or how your back teeth are aligned, you are better off to leave mechanics out of your thoughts during competition. That is what lessons and practice are for. If you execute the right mechanics during practice, it will eventually appear most of the time during a match. If you do not practice proper mechanics, then trying to "make yourself do it" by conscious will power during a match will pretty much ensure a win —- for your opponent.

The most difficult aspect of a post-mortem in sports (or any other human endeavor) is taking an objective view that focuses on what is in your own control. If you think you lost the match because of the rain, or the wind, or your team-mates' shortcomings, you will not improve much in your chosen sports (although you might become proficient at the blame game). If the wind was bothering you, you *could* productively think about how you could better adapt to it next time. If you were playing golf in the rain and hit a lot of shots short, you might conclude that you need to take an extra club in the rain. (Or, you could conclude that the forces of nature are aligned against you because they have nothing better to do. Your choice.) If your tennis doubles partner missed a lot of shots at the net when you were serving, you could day dream about one of the Bryan brothers as your partner. Or, you could focus on getting more and higher quality first serves in. Or, if you really did get a lot of good first serves in, you might think about finding a stronger partner next season. If you pitched a really good softball game but your team lost because of far too many errors, your team practices should include more fielding practice. Just be aware that it is very tempting to blame losses on things that cannot be changed: outside forces, luck, your teammates or even things you cannot change about yourself: "I am just a loser. I am uncoordinated. Blah. Blah." But *all* of these things take you off the hook for *working* on improvements.

Of course, this tendency is not limited to sports. Having read many executive autobiographies, it is amazing how many of them are willing to take full credit when their company does well but any down turns are due to silly government regulations on toxic pollution, or the general business climate or their board of directors, or unfair competition, or the alignment of the moons of Saturn or left-over issues from their predecessors. Those who adopt a more objective look may be less famous but they are definitely more refreshing.

CHAPTER FORTY: PUT IT ALL TOGETHER —
THE MEANING OF LIFE.

According to that most authoritative of sources, *The Hitchhiker's Guide to the Galaxy,* the meaning of life, the universe and everything is forty-two. It is, therefore, fitting to end this book with a chapter that summarizes the advice in this book and place that advice in the context of life, the universe and everything. However, this is chapter forty, not forty-two. Why? I have left two chapters for *you* to write for yourself. Your experience, your body, your enjoyment of sports are all unique. So, the last two chapters are reserved for you to add your own observations, comments, caveats as they apply to your own particular situation.

For this chapter though, let us revisit the title of the book, which by now should have a deeper meaning for you than it did when you first bought it. First, the word "winning" should now have a nuanced meaning. Winning means that you are moving toward achieving your goals, whatever they may be. In turn, this implies that you must take the time and energy to do some self-reflection and discover or invent what your goals are. You need to understand how enjoying sports helps you have a more fulfilling and worthwhile life for *you.*

Second, the word "weekend" is meant to imply that you are limited to some extent in the time that you can devote to your sport or sports. It does not mean that you do not take it "seriously." But it does mean that you have talents in other domains and have chosen one or more of those for your principal means of livelihood or avocation. The more intellectual or sedentary or lacking in competition those other pursuits are, the more important it is to engage in competitive sports to have a well-balanced life.

Third, the word "warrior" is meant to imply that you employ your natural competitive spirit to work hard to achieve your goals *and* that you do this according to a code of honor. In the past, at least, warriors did live by a code of conduct. Of course, you want to "win" in whatever sense that means for you, but you want to accomplish this in such a way that you respect your opponents and the sport itself. You certainly do not want to "destroy" your opponents because then there would be no more opportunity for the sport! Your playing your best is important for them just as their playing their best is important for you. Every sport uses rules, written and unwritten, and it is more important to follow them than it is to score more points. A "victory" won by tallying up more points through cheating is no kind of victory at all. This is no less true in business (or any other aspect of life) than it is in sports. More importantly, sports only serves as a crucial balance to the other aspects of your life if it is based on justice and respect.

Ironically, professional athletes whose livelihood depends on winning often exhibit more grace and good sportsmanship than do a loud and obnoxious minority of weekenders. Some of these latter folks continually question calls, engage in "gamesmanship" to make up for weak fundamentals or play far too aggressively for the situation. For example, in tennis mixed doubles, such a person may try to hit every shot as hard as possible at the woman with the hopes of intimidating her and/or angering her partner. This is not really playing with honor or in the spirit of a true warrior. This is just being a jerk.

On the other hand, in my experience, these "bad apples" are rare. Most "winning weekend warriors" emulate the sportsmanship of professionals and keep the game interesting and fun. Indeed, exceptional sportsmanship positively correlates with exceptional skill. I hope you will excel in both ways and use the tips and techniques in this book to further improve your skill, enjoyment and success!

Go!

ABOUT THE AUTHOR

JOHN CHARLES THOMAS is the author of *The Winning Weekend Warrior.* He has over 200 publications and talks on various topics in the psychology of aging, artificial intelligence and human-computer interaction. He worked most of his life as a research scientist. After earning a Ph.D. at the University of Michigan, he managed a research project on the psychology of aging at Harvard Med School. He then joined IBM Research where he conducted research on human computer interaction. He began and ran an artificial intelligence lab at NYNEX Science and Technology for a dozen years before returning to IBM Research to work on knowledge management, the business use of stories, high performance computing, and cognitive computing. He now lives in Solana Beach, California and is principal of !Problem Solving International, a consulting company focusing on finding, formulating, and solving complex problems.

Learn more about John at www.amazon.com/author/truthtable. You might also enjoy blogs: http://johncharlesthomas.sportsblog.com and https://petersironwood.wordpress.com

REFERENCES

Alexander, C., Ishikawa, S., Silverstein, M., Jacobson, M., Fiksdahl-King, I., Schlomo, A. (1977). *A pattern Language,* Oxford University Press: Cambridge.

Pelz, D. (2000), *Dave Pelz's Putting Bible.* New York, NY

Penick, H. (2012). *Harvey Penick's Little Red Book: Lessons and Teaching from a Lifetime in Golf.* New York, NY: Simon and Schuster.

Rotella, B. & Cullen, B., (1997), *The Golf of Your Dreams.* New York, NY, Simon and Schuster.

Rotella, B. & Clarke, D. (2012), *Golf is not a Game of Perfect.* New York, NY: Simon and Schuster.